Second Edition

Developing an Offensive Game Plan

Brian Billick
Baltimore Ravens

COACHES
CHOICE™

ISBN: 978-1-58518-407-1

Library of Congress Catalog Card Number: 00-110550
Cover design: Paul Lewis
Book layout: Jeanne Hamilton
Cover photo and text photos: Phil Hoffman, courtesy of Baltimore Ravens

Coaches Choice
P.O. Box 1828
Monterey, CA 93942
www.coacheschoice.com

DEDICATION

I would like to thank all the coaches with whom I have worked who have each in some way contributed to the philosophies and concepts presented in this book.

Special thanks to Erica Weiland and Steve Fedie for their help in compiling this material.

FOREWORD

I have had the pleasure of knowing Brian for almost 10 years now, from his days as an offensive coordinator with the Minnesota Vikings, to his present position as head coach of the Baltimore Ravens.

In all of the years we have talked football, one thing in particular has stood out in our conversations. Whatever scenario I present to Brian, whatever question I ask, he has an explanation and reason for his answer.

When you are presenting a game plan to a group of players, you must first believe that everything you are telling them can and will work. Brian does that. He also has taken two very successful offenses: Bill Walsh's "West Coast" offense and Joe Gibb's multiple set, power running game offense, and combined them into one of his own.

It is one thing to have the tools, it is another to get people to understand and use them effectively. This is where I believe Brian's greatest strength lies.

He is extremely organized and takes the approach of a teacher, always holding his students (players) accountable for each and every move and decision they make.

In this book you will learn from one of the brightest offensive minds in football today. He gives you a basic structure of how to put a game plan together, but it will be up to you to get your team to execute like he did in 1998 when the Vikings set an NFL scoring record of 556 points.

You are lucky to be learning from one of the best. I do every time Brian and I talk.

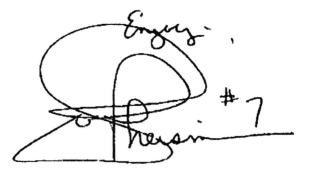

Joe Theismann
World Champion Quarterback

CONTENTS

INTRODUCTION

The purpose of this book is to provide a basic overview of the steps involved in setting up and implementing an offensive game plan. Although the scope of variations facing a coach in high school, college, or professional football can be quite diverse, it is my experience that the basic fundamentals used in installing an offensive structure and game plan remain the same. The primary focus of this book is to outline a very specific structure as to how to determine the size and scope of the offensive scheme you may be using, how to focus that package into a weekly game plan and practice format, and then finally, how to lay out that plan in as direct and simple a manner as possible for both coaches and players.

My coaching experiences range from high school to small and major college to the National Football League. These experiences have shown me that in spite of the unique problems and advantages encountered at each level, the game has certain qualities that carry over from one level to the next.

You should keep in mind that even though the text includes several examples of actual plays from teams I have been associated with that have had success, they serve strictly as examples. It is not my intention to suggest a specific style of play or even a run/pass ratio.

I have had the good fortune to work with several great coaches, including Bill Walsh, Tom Landry, Dan Reeves, Denny Green, and Lavelle Edwards (Brigham Young University). Although each of these successful coaches was very different in his personality and approach to the game, there were two constants about each: 1) they were all excellent teachers; and 2) all of these individuals had a very well-defined structure to which they adhere in preparing their teams. It is those two constants, above all else, that I have tried to maintain in my coaching career. This commitment, coupled with the viewpoints of the many talented coaches with whom I have had the good fortune to work, is what I have based my philosophies on when I was the offensive coordinator of the Minnesota Vikings and as the head coach of the Baltimore Ravens, and which I have outlined in this book.

Even though the situation with which you are working may vary a great deal from the problems I face in the National Football League, it is my hope that by outlining the way we approach our game plan preparation, you may be able to apply some of these principles or formulas to the preparation of your team. For discussion purposes in this book, I will refer to your responsibility of preparing a game plan as that of the offensive coordinator. I understand that this nomenclature may not be the specific title you hold. On the other hand, whether you are performing these duties as the head coach while serving as your own play caller, or you simply have not been given the title, "offensive coordinator" best describes those responsibilities.

Define Your Job

One of the first things you should do is to identify what exactly your job as the offensive coordinator is. I learned quite early in my career that the job should be taken quite literally. The title of the job is offensive "coordinator," not offensive "genius," not offensive "guru," and not offensive "mastermind."

The dictionary defines the word "coordinate" as: to arrange in proper order, harmonious adjustment, or interaction. I think the key word in this definition is "interaction." This interaction happens on two levels. First, you must be able to interact effectively with the other members of your offensive staff. We have had the opportunity over the years to work with an excellent group of coaches, each with a wide variety of experiences and capabilities. It would be foolish to not utilize those capabilities by excluding them from the creation and implementation of our game plans. Secondly, the most brilliant of game plans is useless unless it can be readily learned and executed by your players. To this end, how you install and practice your game plan is almost as, if not more, important than the selection of plays you come up with.

In an interview published in the January 1993 issue of the *Harvard Business Review*, Bill Walsh outlined many of his philosophical approaches to the preparation of his many successful football teams. In that piece he stated, "*A system should never reduce the game to the point where it simply blames the players for failure because they did not physically overwhelm the opponent.*" Coach Walsh went on to say, "*You need to have a plan even for the worst scenario. It doesn't mean that it will always be successful. But you will always be prepared and at your best.*"

At any level, you must sell your game plan every week to your players so they are confident in what is being run and are enthusiastic about the opportunities they will have by implementing your game plan. The more your players can gain a sense of confidence that they are prepared for anything that might come up, the less likely they are to feel "physically overwhelmed," even if their opponent is capable of doing just that.

As a Teacher

In arranging your game plan in "harmonious order or adjustment," it must be done in an atmosphere that maximizes the "learning curve" of your players. There is little secret that players do not perform at their best when hesitation exists in their minds about what is expected of them.

It has been proven time and again, both statistically and in practical application, that 60 minutes is *not always* enough time for the *best team* to win. It is *just enough* time for the team that *plays the best* to win. As a coach, you will not catch a single pass, throw a single block, or score a single touchdown this season. Nor will you, on a consistent basis, make that singularly brilliant play call that wins the game.

Football is a game with very defined parameters. The very nature of the game and the geometric relationship of the field to the distances required to move the ball are very specific and definable. The exciting part of coaching for me is knowing I can affect the game by providing as much information as possible to my team in preparing them for what they will face during the course of a game.

In his book, *The Road Ahead*, Microsoft founder Bill Gates defines "information" as the *"reduction of uncertainty."* In other words, from a football perspective, the information you provide your offensive personnel must reduce their uncertainty as much as possible, if you expect them to execute your game plan with confidence and without hesitation or uncertainty.

This is not to say you can "program" any specific player to be better than he is. I often tell my players that there are two types of players I *cannot* have: One is a player who *cannot do* what he is told, the other is a player who *can only do* exactly what he is told. At some point the players' God-given talents, character, and drive to succeed must take control. However, you as a coach have a responsibility to provide those players with information and a structure that will allow their abilities to flourish.

I have no delusions about the offensive success we had with the Vikings during my last few years in Minnesota. With players like Warren Moon, Chris Carter, Jake Reed, Amp Lee, and Randall McDaniel, it was clearly the talents and character of these types of players that was the cornerstone of the record-breaking production. I can, however, take a great deal of satisfaction in knowing that we coaches had, at the very least, provided a platform for those great athletes to accomplish what they did.

One of the secrets to providing this information is to consolidate the amount of information players have to process into a workable, learnable level. It is quite evident that players today are products of the "video generation." As such, materials presented to them must "grab" their attention in a manner in which they are accustomed. Simply standing up at a chalkboard and bludgeoning them with your game plan is not optimizing the "learning curve" to which your players are used.

Accordingly, as a coach/teacher, it is your responsibility to continually search for new and innovative ways to provide your players with the information they need. If the game has changed in the last few years, it has been less in terms of the fundamental approach to the X's and O's than in the technological ways this information is prepared.

Many coaches, particularly young coaches coming into the profession, are finding a number of creative and helpful ways to use personal computers in the analysis and preparation of football-related materials. Although some coaches are still uncomfortable with this technology and therefore dismiss it as being too fancy for their needs, the use of computers can enhance your production just like it has in any number of other professions. It is a very effective way to analyze and present a large amount of information in a more concise and organized manner.

I believe the computer is one of the best "teaching" tools available to you. Much like the use of video when compared to film, the advances in available technology can make a big difference in presenting your materials to your players. Accordingly, this book includes several examples of how the Vikings, when I was on Minnesota's staff, used computers to analyze and present materials to our team. Most of these methods are available to you by means of the simplest of computer programs in the form of spreadsheets (Excel, Lotus...), word processing (Word Perfect, Microsoft Word...), or drawing programs (Super Paint, Visio...). How these teaching aids can be used by coaches is discussed in more detail later in this book.

Elements of Preparation

The process of developing an offensive game plan will be examined in four main areas:

- Determine the size and scope of the offense
- Outline your situational offensive needs
- Implementations of the game plan
- Game-day needs

First, the book looks at how much offense your team will need in any given year, week, or game. Determining the size of your offensive package is the most fundamental of questions that must be answered before you can begin to formulate an offensive game plan.

Once these parameters have been established, the book examines the actual elements that make up each segment of "situational offense" that you must account for in a game plan. This step is broken down in the following manner:

- Base offense
- Third down
- Pre-Red Zone
- Red Zone
- Special categories

Each situational area is then discussed and outlined as to its size, scope, and special considerations. Next, how the game plan is formulated and presented to the team is examined, and what allocation of time should be given to each situational area in meetings and practice. Finally, the review of the game-plan layout will address the way in which the game plan that has been selected is laid out and implemented on game day.

How Does This Apply to You

In each of these sections, the materials are discussed with regards to the way the Minnesota Vikings approached each situation when I was on the Vikings' staff, with the Vikings' desired ratio of run to pass, drop back to play action, zone protection vs. man protection, inside running game vs. outside running game, etc. These examples are just that—examples. It is not the intent of this book to advocate a particular style of play, but to outline a structured approach to implement your offense, whatever your particular philosophy may be.

The phrase "West Coast Offense" is probably one of the most popular and yet misused phrases in the coaching lexicon today. Many people think of it as a specific style of runs or passes that emulates the success of the San Francisco 49ers during the 1980s and into the '90s. Although this style of play can be traced as far back as Sid Gilman and Paul Brown of the early AFL days, it was clearly Bill Walsh who consolidated and refined the basic concepts of this philosophy.

However, when I think of Bill Walsh and the "West Coast Offense", I think less of his actual X's and O's than I do of the comprehensive approach Coach Walsh took to creating an offensive structure. That structure was based on specific teaching methods that carried a team systematically from installing the offense in training camp, to weekly installation of the game plans and practices, to the actual implementation of the game plan on game day. It is this systematic approach, that I learned from people like Bill Walsh and Dennis Green, that I am attempting to convey in this book. Regardless of the style of play you advocate, the overall structure of preparing your team through the game plan remains the same.

Measurable Probabilities

As the important parameters of situational offense are reviewed in this book, you should keep in mind a couple of focal points that have a direct effect on the outcome of a game. A number of studies that focused on probability and statistical measures have been conducted over the last two decades in the NFL that attempted to devlop a valid shortlist of priorities in which the team winning a game was significantly more productive than the team that lost that particular game.

Although research suggests that any number of variables can and will intervene to affect performance and the outcome of a game, over the last few years a clear-cut pattern has been established. From year to year, four factors have been identified that consistently have a high correlation to a team's winning or losing:

- Turnovers
- Explosive plays
- First-down efficiency
- Red Zone efficiency

Turnovers have long been recognized as a major determinant of the outcome of a game. A team with a positive turnover ratio in any given game has between a 75-85% better chance of winning a game than its opponent. This is an interactive measurable because it has to do with the giveaway-takeaway relationship of both offense and defense. The advantage of a team who has a high takeaway margin is negated if its offense is giving up the ball at the same ratio, and vice versa.

Explosive plays are measured by the NFL as gains of 20 yards or more. A more detailed analysis shows a more valid measure being runs of 12 yards or more and passes of 16 yards or more. These levels of production proved to be more significant as to what is needed to constitute and gain the effects of an "explosion". The 1994 and '95 NFL seasons were the first in a dozen years that explosions carried a higher winning ratio than did turnovers. This measurement showed that a team with a +2 or greater advantage won the game between 80-85% of the time. The significant thing about explosives is that they do not necessarily need to lead to a score to be productive. Huge changes of field position can also positively change the profile of a game. This measurement, like turnovers, is an interactive measurable because a team's effectiveness in this area can be diminished if your defense is giving up explosives at the same rate as the offense is gaining them.

1st-down (+4 yds.) efficiency has a direct effect on your ability to stay on schedule with your play calling by maintaining a 3rd and medium-to-short ratio as much as possible. The two keys to this measurable are running effectively on first down (about 45%) and completing a high percentage of passes (better than 60%).

The range or efficiency in this situation will run between 40-50%. Although this factor does not appear to be a huge difference from the worst teams to the best, it is significant when you consider that your first down calls constitute between 40-45% of your total plays run in a year. These percentages may seem low to you with regards to being highly effective, but a closer look at the top first-down efficiency teams in the NFL in 1995 will show you how consistent these levels are:

TEAM	1ST DOWNS	+4 PLAYS	%
VIKINGS	490	238	49%
BEARS	467	232	50%
DOLPHINS	472	232	50%
49ERS	480	232	49%

Red Zone efficiency (percentage of scores vs. number of series) becomes an important measurable because you are talking about scores. The key point to make in this instance is the importance of scoring any points — touchdowns or field goals — as being efficient. This factor will be discussed in much more detail in the chapter dealing with the Red Zone.

A perfect example of how these measurable categories can have a direct effect on the ability of a team to win was the Vikings' 1993 season. That season was a transition year for us with the loss of three of our starting five offensive linemen from the Central Division Championship team of 1992. In addition, we had a new quarterback in Jim McMahon. We also lost Terry Allen, a 1,000-yard rusher the previous season, during the pre-season.

In spite of this, we were able to win four of our last five games (against four playoff teams and three division winners) to earn a spot in the playoffs. We were able to accomplish this by being among the top teams in the NFL in three of the four measurable categories: 1st-down efficiency, turnovers, and Red Zone efficiency. In 1993, the Vikings ranked fourth in the NFL in 1st-down +4 efficiency, fourth in the League in fewest turnovers, and first in the NFL in Red Zone efficiency at 96%.

Although you have to be concerned with many variables in establishing your play calling, we have found that these four measurable categories are significant enough to warrant considerable attention. As such, these measurable categories are periodically referred to throughout the book when priorities for each offensive situation are discussed.

Summary Points

The key elements in designing and developing your offensive package are:

*   Define your job as "offensive coordinator" and the approach you will take.

*   Recognize that above all else you are a teacher and determine the capabilities of your students/players and the best methods of teaching/coaching them.

*   Focus on four main elements when preparing any game plan:

    ✓ Determining the size and scope of the offense
    ✓ Outlining your situational offensive needs
    ✓ Implementation of the game plan
    ✓ Game-day needs

*   Remember that the number one factor in approaching each of the aforementioned four elements is to be as detailed and specific as your time and materials allow.

*   Keep the four "key" measurable categories in mind when formulating your game plan:

    ✓ Turnovers
    ✓ Explosive plays
    ✓ First-down efficiency
    ✓ Red Zone efficiency

CHAPTER 1

How Much Offense?

Two of the most fundamental questions you need to ask are:

- How much offense can my team run during a season?

- How much offense can be effectively practiced and run each week?

Keep in mind that the amount of offense you can handle may be vastly different than what your players can handle. As any teacher knows, you must teach/coach to your least common denominator.

Part of your job as offensive coordinator is to make sure you are using the plays and techniques that best fit the abilities of your players. Your specific situation and how you deal with it may change from year to year based on the turnover of your personnel. In the NFL, we are now dealing with the same problems of player turnover that those of coaches at the high school and collegiate levels have been facing their entire careers. With the advent of free agency in the NFL, most teams are experiencing a 20-25% yearly turnover. Mathematically at least, an NFL team (like their interscholastic and intercollegiate counterparts) could have a total roster turnover every four years. Although certain key NFL players (like a quarterback) may be tied up contractually for longer periods of time, the turnover of the rest of the offense is something an NFL coach has to consider every year when determining how much offense the team can carry over from one year to the next.

Regardless of what type of team you coach (interscholastic, college, professional, or youth), you must think on three levels when determining the amount of offense with which you can deal:

- Yearly
- Weekly
- Game day

Each level has very set parameters as to how much offense will actually be run in any given segment. The more you can overlap the amount of total offense you can carry vs. the amount that can be effectively practiced, the more effective the offense you actually run on game day will be.

It is impossible to accurately predict the exact amount of offense you will use in any given game. There is always going to be a certain amount of overage that has to be built in for the "what if's". For example, "what if" they blitz more than you had thought?; "what if" you aren't able to run the ball as well as you thought?; "what if" your quarterback is having an off day?; or "what if" the weather is bad?

We have tried to keep our overage to between 25-30 percent of the total game snaps we can predict. This percentage of overage is something we work very hard to maintain. Each week, I examine how much of the offensive game plan was actually used vs. what was installed and practiced, looking to see if our offensive game plan can be pared down.

On the other hand, you have to be careful about not limiting yourself too much. Many coaches may try to eliminate too much offense because it makes less for them to have to prepare. You don't want to waste time working on things you are never going to use, but you must have all that you need to get the job done.

Diagram 1-1 provides a diagram key that can be utilized to help illustrate the various offensive game-plan and actual game-play ratios:

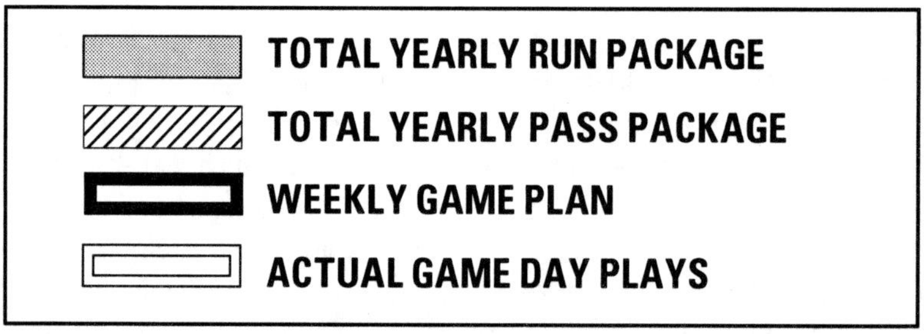

TOTAL YEARLY RUN PACKAGE

TOTAL YEARLY PASS PACKAGE

WEEKLY GAME PLAN

ACTUAL GAME DAY PLAYS

Diagram 1-1. Graphic key for offensive package (yearly, weekly, actual) ratios.

Diagram 1-2 represents a basic offensive package that is balanced between runs and passes. In this example, the game-plan and actual game-day calls fell within the expected norms that were set going into the game. This situation is obviously a winning profile when the amount of offense practiced and used match each other very well.

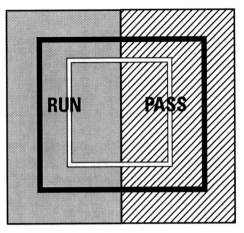

Diagram 1-2.

Diagrams 1-3 and 1-4 represent the same offense but with a different game plan. In this example, the game plan calls for the passing game to be a little more prominent, possibly because your opponent plays really good run defense, or perhaps because their secondary is highly vulnerable. Diagram 1-3 shows that the game went according to your plan, and you were able to throw the ball effectively

Diagram 1-4 is an example of the same approach; but once you actually played the game, you found you were able to run the ball more effectively than you thought and pushed that aspect of the game plan more. Again, both examples showed you planned well, were very efficient in your preparation, and were able to stay with your basic game plan.

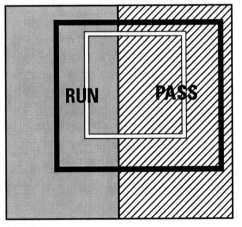

Diagram 1-3.

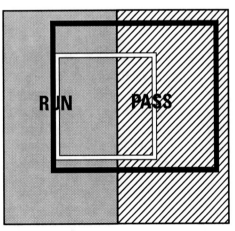

Diagram 1-4.

Diagrams 1-5 and 1-6 are examples of the same game plans by a team whose base game plan this week is focused more on the run.

In Diagram 1-5, the game plan went according to schedule with the run being the main focus. In Diagram 1-6, that same game plan obviously could not establish the run the way it was designed. Not only did this team have to rely more on the pass, but it was forced to draw on part of its base passing attack that was not practiced during the week.

Ideally, you would like to keep this type of play calling to a minimum. Often, however, there may be a base part of your attack that you have used enough during the year that even though you may not have emphasized it during the week, you are still comfortable coming back to it in any given game.

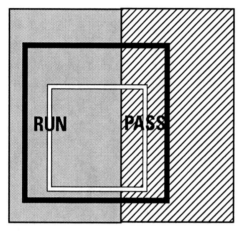

Diagram 1-5.

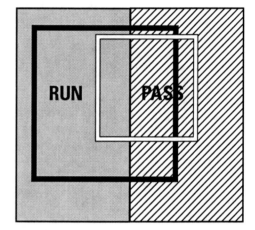

Diagram 1-6.

Diagrams 1-7 and 1-8 show the approach of a team whose primary yearly offensive structure is based more on the run. In Diagram 1-7, the game plan obviously went according to plan.

Diagram 1-8 is an example of a game we would all like to avoid. This example shows that the base game-day calls were not effective, and you had to go to other aspects of the offense that were not emphasized during the week. Furthermore, you apparently got desperate enough you had to make things up as you went along, outside of your basic offensive structure. Obviously if you find yourself in this situation too often, you must go back and re-examine whether you are using the best offense available for your personnel, and also re-examine the way you are selecting and practicing your game plans.

You should keep these examples in mind as you look at the size and scope of the offense you want to develop, both as a whole and in certain situations. I think it will become quite clear to you what we are talking about when the parameters are discussed of how much your offensive package, weekly game plans, and game-day calls encompass.

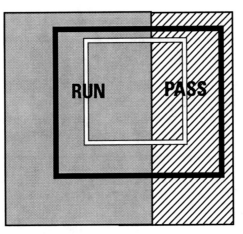

Diagram 1-7.

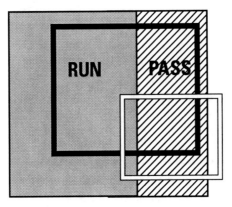

Diagram 1-8.

Numbers of Plays

To help determine the size of your offensive package (yearly, weekly and game day), some parameters need to be set with regard to the actual number of plays run in a game. Again, keep in mind that the examples provided in this book are based on statistics involving the Minnesota Vikings and the NFL. Figure 1-1 illustrates the offensive circumstances of seven different NFL teams for the 1995 season. Presenting an overview of the variances between teams and specific situations, this cross section of examples uses teams from different conferences and divisions, different styles of play, and different success rates. In spite of the differences, it is easy to see how consistent the play ratios remain.

As Figure 1-1 shows, all of these teams ran slightly more plays than the NFL average. The average number of total plays run in a year in the NFL during the 1994 and 1995 seasons was 986 (1994) and 997 (1995), or about 62 plays a game. Compare these numbers with the Vikings' overall numbers during the four-year period (1992-95) that are detailed in Figure 1-2. Again, you can see how similar the ratios are, even though there was a great difference between the production and style of our 1992-93 season and the 1994-95 seasons.

As Figure 1-2 illustrates, the Minnesota Vikings ran 1076 (1994) and 1081 (1995) plays for the third and sixth highest totals during that period. This number averages out to about 68 and 67 plays a game, respectively. During that same period, Tampa Bay ran 905 (1995) plays for the lowest number of plays in the NFL, averaging 56 plays a game.

OVERALL	MINN	DENVER	CHICAGO	GREEN BAY	PITTS	SAN DIEGO	WASH	TEAM AVG	PER GAME
1ST DOWN	465	441	480	482	480	440	454	463	28.9
2ND LONG	224	214	195	228	229	238	233	223	13.9
2ND MED	122	111	132	111	120	87	100	112	7.0
2ND 1	24	33	20	20	19	26	13	22	1.4
3RD 11+	42	32	17	28	35	35	39	33	2.0
3RD 7-10	70	86	74	80	71	80	99	80	5.0
3RD 4-6	62	48	61	51	65	64	57	58	3.6
3RD 2-3	34	30	30	49	32	32	36	35	2.2
3RD 1	33	28	33	26	26	15	14	25	1.6
4TH	10	19	22	6	26	19	17	17	1.1
	1,086	1,042	1,064	1,081	1,103	1,036	1,062	1,068	66.7

Figure 1-1. The number of plays dealing with specific situations by selected NFL teams during the 1995 season.

OVERALL	1992	1993	1994	1995	TEAM AVG	PER GAME
1ST DOWN	420	417	458	465	440	27.50
2ND LONG	216	206	241	224	222	13.88
2ND MED	95	115	113	122	111	6.94
2ND 1	27	19	15	24	21	1.31
3RD 11+	27	36	30	42	34	2.13
3RD 7-10	56	66	94	70	72	4.50
3RD 4-6	50	50	40	62	51	3.19
3RD 2-3	42	36	46	34	40	2.50
3RD 1	34	25	25	33	29	1.81
4TH	9	5	14	10	10	0.63
	976	975	1,076	1,086	1,030	64

Figure 1-2. The number of plays run by the Minnesota Vikings during the period 1992-'95 that deal with specific offensive situations.

In 1992 and 1993, the Vikings were a much more run-oriented team and finished 13th and 11th in the NFL in total offense. During the period, three different quarterbacks and six different running backs started at one time or another. As was discussed earlier, our base offense (run/pass ratio) was dramatically different for those two years than the next two.

During the two-year period (1994-'95) when the Vikings finished third and fourth in total offense in the NFL, respectively, the averages were obviously pushed up. These numbers need to be broken down further if we are to examine the size and scope of our game-plan discussions (Figure 1-3).

OPEN FIELD:	1992	1993	1994	1995	AVG	PER GAME	
1ST SERIES	162	159	167	163	163	10.17	
1ST 10+	5	12	15	19	13	0.80	
1ST EARNED	156	161	177	179	168	10.52	
1ST 9-	1	0	1	2	1	0.06	
2ND LONG	175	162	189	174	175	10.94	
2ND MED	69	88	84	77	80	4.97	
2ND 1	14	11	9	17	13	0.80	
3RD 11+	20	33	26	30	27	1.70	
3RD 7-10	46	48	66	55	54	3.36	
3RD 4-6	39	33	35	46	38	2.39	
3RD 2-3	29	26	30	20	26	1.64	
3RD 1	24	16	17	22	20	1.23	
4TH	5	4	5	3	4	0.27	49
RED ZONE:							
1ST SERIES	9	7	4	12	8	0.50	
1ST 10+	2	1	4	3	3	0.16	
1ST EARNED	60	51	70	63	61	3.81	
1ST GOAL	25	26	20	24	24	1.48	
2ND LONG	41	44	52	50	47	2.92	
2ND MED	26	27	29	45	32	1.98	
2ND 1	13	8	6	7	9	0.53	
3RD 11+	7	3	4	12	7	0.41	
3RD 7-10	10	18	28	15	18	1.11	
3RD 4-6	11	17	5	16	12	0.77	
3RD 2-3	13	10	16	14	13	0.83	
3RD 1	10	9	7	11	10	0.59	
4TH	4	1	9	7	5	0.33	15
TOTAL PLAYS	976	975	1,076	1,086	1,028	64	

Figure 1-3. The number of play calls by year dealing with specific open-field vs. Red Zone situations by the Minnesota Vikings.

The values in these situational breakdowns are what we will use in our discussion in each area about the amount of offense needed. The averages in each area can help us set the parameters for the size of the offensive package we need and ultimately the amount of offense we will use each week. These numbers stay amazingly consistent from year to year and even from team to team. Using the same seven teams from the earlier overall example, Figure 1-4 illustrates this consistency.

OPEN FIELD:	MINN	DENVER	CHICAGO	GREEN BAY	PITTS	SAN DIEGO	WASH	TEAM AVG	PER GAME
1ST DOWN	363	350	356	378	370	354	355	361	22.6
2ND LONG	174	177	152	184	178	195	185	178	11.1
2ND MED	77	76	84	80	80	64	70	76	4.7
2ND 1	17	23	13	14	9	19	7	15	0.9
3RD 11+	30	29	16	27	26	23	32	26	1.6
3RD 7-10	55	70	55	63	47	64	80	62	3.9
3RD 4-6	46	31	37	38	47	56	39	42	2.6
3RD 2-3	20	21	24	30	24	17	19	22	1.4
3RD 1	22	17	23	19	21	11	9	17	1.1
4TH	3	13	13	3	10	13	7	9	0.6
									50.6

RED ZONE	MINN	DENVER	CHICAGO	GREEN BAY	PITTS	SAN DIEGO	WASH	TEAM AVG	PER GAME
1ST DOWN	78	63	79	74	75	63	74	72	4.5
2ND LONG	50	37	43	44	51	43	48	45	2.8
2ND MED	45	35	48	31	40	23	30	36	2.3
2ND 1	7	10	7	6	10	7	6	8	0.5
3RD 11+	13	3	1	1	9	12	7	6	0.4
3RD 7-10	15	16	19	17	24	16	19	18	1.1
3RD 4-6	16	17	24	13	18	8	18	16	1.0
3RD 2-3	14	9	6	19	8	15	17	13	0.8
3RD 1	11	11	10	7	5	4	5	8	0.5
4TH	7	6	9	3	16	6	10	8	0.5
1ST GOAL	24	28	45	30	35	23	25	30	1.9
									16.3

Figure 1-4. Offensive situational breakdowns by selected NFL teams.

Your actual numbers will vary by the level of play, the number of games played in a year, and to a small degree, the type of offense you run. The differences usually are no more than 10-15%. In Figure 1-5, a breakdown of the same ratios by the 1989-91 Stanford University teams shows similar results.

Most college teams, however, traditionally run more plays during a game. For example, in 1995, the average major college team ran 795 plays, over 11 games, for an average of about 72 plays a game.

As is usually the case with statistics, they can be very accurate, yet completely wrong at the same time. The average American family, for example, consists of 2.3 children. This statistic is completely accurate. However, how many families do you know that have exactly 2.3 children? Get my point? While these numbers can be very helpful in determining ratios and parameters, you should keep in mind that every team and game is different, and there are going to be "anticipated" fluctuations from game to game.

OPEN FIELD:				STANFORD	
	1989	1990	1991	YEARLY AVG	AVG PER GAME
1ST DOWN	138	142	135	138	13
1ST EARNED	152	152	148	151	14
2ND LONG	149	133	136	139	13
2ND MED	68	69	62	66	6
2ND 1	12	12	11	12	1
3RD 7+	65	63	52	60	5
3RD 4-6	34	52	52	46	4
3RD 2-3	24	26	21	24	2
3RD 1	12	11	10	11	1
4TH	4	10	3	6	1

Figure 1-5. Offensive situational breakdown for Stanford University during one three-year period, 1989-'91.

In subsequent chapters in this book, these numbers and ratios are referred to a good deal in outlining the amount of offense you need to account for in each offensive situational category.

Summary Points

The key elements in determining how much offense you should carry are:

- Think on three levels in determining how much offense you can run: yearly, weekly and on game day.

- Take the time to determine exactly the size and scope of each critical situation you will face.

- Work hard to keep your overage of plays to 25-30%.

- Take the time to review each week the amount and nature of offense you ran and see if your planning stayed within the expected norms you set for yourself.

CHAPTER 2

Base Offense

Developing an offensive game plan begins, quite naturally, with our open-field base offense. This task is undertaken with particular attention given to our "openers." As we do with all the situational sections in this book, we first examine the amount of offense we will need in this section.

Based on the open-field segment of your game plan, first down requires about 45% of your total calls in the open field. Second down involve about 35%, while third and fourth downs collectively take up the remaining 20%. Our base package encompasses all first and second downs.

OPEN FIELD:	1992	1993	1994	1995	AVG	PER
1ST SERIES	162	159	167	163	163	10
1ST 10+	5	12	15	19	13	1
1ST EARNED	156	161	177	179	168	11
1ST 9-	1	0	1	2	1	1
2ND LONG	175	162	189	174	175	11
2ND MED	69	88	84	77	80	5
2ND 1	14	11	9	17	13	1

Figure 2-1. Situational breakdowns of the base package of the Minnesota Vikings' offensive game plan during the period 1992-'95.

As you can see in Figure 2-1, our first-down package typically consists of about 23-25 calls per game; 2nd-and-long (7+ yds.) constitutes about 11-12 calls per game, while second-and-medium (2-6 yds.) occurs only about 5-6 times per game. Finally, second-and-1 in the open field usually comes up only once a game. It is quite evident that your first downs to open a series and earned first downs take up most of the first-down calls. First-and-10+ or first-and-less-than-10 (usually first-and-5 after a penalty) are speciality calls that are discussed later. Equally as evident is the fact that the number of second-and-long calls are usually double that of second-and-medium.

One of the first analyses you will want to do is to determine if your opponent significantly separates its defensive scheme from a first-down situation to a second-and-long scenario. Many teams will just continue their base calls from first down into second-and-long, while others will change their coverage package to accommodate the long down and distance. Still other defensive teams may actually blitz more in this situation because they anticipate more passing on your part.

Certainly, if a defensive team just continues its normal defensive posture in second-and-long, it allows more carryover and more continuity if you can simply extend your first-down package into the 10-12 plays of second-and-long. It is my experience that most teams have a separate package for their second-and-medium calls. This down and distance is a more advantageous situation for the offense because the offense has a much better chance to remain balanced with run, pass, and play actions and still get a first down.

Although a good deal more pressure exists in making your third-down calls, I find third-down offense one of the simpler areas for which to prepare. Like any other offensive situation, the number of plays you will need are very defined. Furthermore, most defenses have very specific and identifiable packages on third down.

The average team in the NFL faces about between 200-220 third-down situations a year. That averages out to about 12-14 calls a game. On the average, 10 of those will fall in the open field, while 2-4 will be needed in the Red Zone.

The distance a team has to go on third down also varies substantially. Typical third-down-and-distance ratios are shown in Figure 2-2.

OPEN FIELD:	1992	1993	1994	1995	AVG	PER
3RD 11+	20	33	26	30	27	2
3RD 7-10	46	48	66	55	54	3
3RD 4-6	39	33	35	46	38	2
3RD 2-3	29	26	30	20	26	2
3RD 1	24	16	17	22	20	1

Figure 2-2. Typical third-down-and-distance breakdowns during an NFL game.

The purpose and approach we take by breaking third down up in this manner is discussed later in the third-down chapter. For more basic purposes, third down is simply categorized into three areas by yardage: long (7+), medium (2-6) and short (1).

During the two-year period (1994-'95), the Vikings faced 241 and 239 third-down situations, respectively. This was a good news/bad news scenario. The good news is you are generating a great deal of offense; the bad news is that by producing this many plays, you have forced yourself into more critical third-down calls.

A direct correlation exists between the number of total plays run and the number of third-down plays. This correlation is one of the most consistent variables in the NFL, with virtually every team falling between the norms. Regardless of whether a team is good or bad, a passing team or a running team, all teams face a third-down conversion every fourth or fifth play of a series.

NFL	AVG TOTAL PLAYS	AVG #3RD DOWNS	PER
1995	997	218	4.57
1994	989	219	4.52
1993	968	215	4.50
1992	918	204	4.50

Figure 2-3. The number of third-down plays, relative to total number of plays run in the game.

Having worked through this long maze of numbers, we can now put them together to identify exactly what our starting point is for developing an offensive game plan and how we can build our game plan from there.

Number of Plays Needed

What we have seen to this point is that very specific and unidentifiable parameters exist within which we can isolate how much offense is required in each situational offense category. Table 2-1 shows the numbers broken down and the situations we have discussed so far.

It is relatively easy to see how we have reached a point where we can identify the specific number and type of plays with which we want to begin our game plan. Take first down as the initial example. We start with the recognition that we will be making about 20 first-down calls in the open field. We then cut that in half to start with the 10 opening first-half, open-field calls.

	1ST DOWN	2ND LONG	2ND MED	2ND SHORT	3RD LONG	3RD MED	3RD SHORT
TOTAL PLAYS	20	10	5	1	5	5	1
1ST HALF PLAYS	10	5	3	1	3	3	1
RUNS	5	2	2	1		1	1
DROP BACK	2	2			3	1	
QUICKS	1	1				1	
PLAY ACTION	2		1	1			1

Table 2-1. Game-plan ratio chart for the open field.

In this example, if you have a team that strives to have a balanced run/pass ratio on first down, you should break your first-down openers into five runs and five passes. In a second-and-long situation, if you would like to maintain at least a 70/30 pass/run ratio and would prefer a 60/40 split, you should script five plays for the first half—three passes and two runs. Because a second-and-medium situation constitutes about five plays a game, we script three for the first half with a two-to-one run/pass ratio.

Furthermore, you may have have decided that you want your opening passes to be two dropbacks, one quick, and two play actions. If this philosophy and thinking is applied to all the open-field situations, you will end up with the total opening-play agenda that is shown in Figure 2-4.

RUNS:	12
PASSES:	16
DROP BACK:	8
QUICKS:	3
PLAY ACTION:	5

Figure 2-4. Breakdowns of opening plays.

Using our opening 12 runs as an example, two of them will likely be in short-yardage situations and may in fact be the same play. Likewise, the run we have scheduled for 3rd-and-long may be the same run we intend for 3rd-and-medium. That being the case, that leaves you with 10 opening runs. Those 10 runs do not have to be 10 different plays. More likely they would be three or four different runs from two or three different formations. Furthermore, it would stand to reason that we would want to build the five play-action passes off those runs and formations.

Of the three quicks we choose to throw, we may want to link them to two of the formations from which we are throwing our eight dropback passes, or to one or two of the run formations, and so on. How much carryover you wish to have from your first- and second-down plays to your third-down calls is certainly up to you. You may want to draw from your base throws and simply change the formations, or you may want to give them a complete new set of plays.

Once you have established the priority of your opening plays, you can expand on that package to the point of even doubling those initial 30 plays to have a base open-field package of 60 plays, with your average 50 open-field calls coming from that package. This approach certainly fits within the limits we set earlier of about 20% overage in your preparation.

I want to reemphasize that these ratios are examples of a particular offensive philosophy. While the approach can remain the same, the specific run/pass ratio you employ can be whatever fits your offensive package.

Figure 2-5 illustrates a profile of the team we saw earlier in the introduction section of this book that bases its offensive package on a more run-oriented emphasis. In that regard, the opening sequence ratio of the team in Table 2-2 shows that this team clearly has established its intention to run the ball more and subsequently throw more play-action passes than drop-back passes. This same approach can be applied in the Red Zone where the remaining 25% (18 plays) of your offense will be called. These ratios and the approach we take in each situational area are discussed in subsequent chapters that address those specific areas of emphasis.

Breaking your play selection down to this specific focus allows you to be very detailed about what it is you want to run and how each play can work in relationship to each other. This approach is the basis for establishing your "openers".

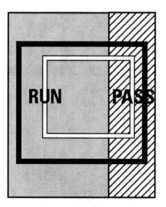

Figure 2-5. An example of a team with a run-oriented offensive package.

	1ST DOWN	2ND LONG	2ND MED	2ND SHORT	3RD LONG	3RD MED	3RD SHORT
TOTAL PLAYS	20	10	5	1	5	5	1
1ST HALF PLAYS	10	5	3	1	3	3	1
RUNS	7	3	2	1	1	1	1
DROP BACK		1			3		
QUICKS	1	1				1	
PLAY ACTION	2		1	1		1	1

RUNS:	16
PASSES:	12
DROPBACK:	4
QUICKS:	3
PLAY ACTION:	6

Table 2-2. An example of a team's opening sequence ratio.

Openers

Considerable interest has been focused on the concept of "openers," whether it be the famous "25 Openers" Bill Walsh utilized, to the programmed shifting and motioning of Joe Gibbs' Redskins teams. What the concept of openers boils down to is a very specific and detailed approach to your opening game plan. As far back as 1979 at the American Football Coach Association National Convention, Bill Walsh — in his clinic talk, "Controlling the Ball with the Passing Game" — labeled the establishing of your openers as "the single most valuable thing that a coach can do as far as the game plan is concerned." At a minimum, establishing your openers should accomplish the following nine purposes:

Allows you to make decisions in the cool and calm of your office during the week after a thorough analysis of your opponent.

This philosophy is the basis from which the entire offense and game-plan structure should evolve. It recognizes that even the best of game-day coaches must plan ahead for all possible contingencies if the problems that a team will inevitably face each week are going to be handled effectively. In the *Harvard Business Review* article by Bill Walsh that was cited earlier, Walsh stated, "Making judgments under severe stress is the most difficult thing there is. The more preparation you have prior to the conflict, the more you can do in a clinical situation, the better off you will be. I want to make certain that we have accounted for every critical situation."

Allows you to determine a desirable pass/run ratio.

We work very hard at maintaining an equal balance on first down between running and passing. This down is one of the few situations on which the defense has to guess somewhat regarding what your run/pass ratio may be. In 1995, the open-field, first-down pass/run ratio by the Vikings' main personnel groupings looked like this:

Personnel	Pass	Run
• Two backs/one tight end/two wide outs	70	67
• One back/one tight end/two wide outs	54	53
• Two backs/three wide outs	14	14

The only way to consistently maintain this type of 50/50 balance is through effectively scripting such a ratio through your openers. Keep in mind that there is nothing wrong with having tendencies. Anything you do well is going to have a certain level of predictability. Too many coaches talk themselves out of running certain things just because they know the defense knows what is coming. You should make your opponent prove they can stop a strength before you change what you do just to go against your tendencies. A world of difference exists between being predictable because you are unaware of a tendency and doing what you do best and making a defense show you they can stop you.

Allows you to make full usage of formations and personnel by making the run and pass interactive.

By controlling the sequencing of your openers, you can be much more detailed in creating legitimate play action and action passes from formation and personnel groupings that will be used early in the game plan. This step also gives those players who have a limited role in the offense (but have a certain number of plays they are being counted on to help run) an opportunity to see exactly what and where they have a chance to contribute.

Gives you a chance to challenge the defense and see what adjustments the defense may have incorporated into the defensive game plan, based on your different formations and personnel.

Openers are an excellent way to test the defense to see what the defense's game plan is, based on your formations and personnel. By anticipating what those adjustments might be, you can then expand on those things you think will be successful based on the defense's adjustments. If you have an idea of how the defense is going to adjust to a certain motion and have a play that has "explosive" potential, you may script a more basic play in your openers from that same motion to reconfirm that the defense is indeed going to react the way you anticipated.

Gives your assistant coaches a specific focus as to what is being run and what they should watch for.

This factor is one of the most important reasons for establishing your openers and making sure the rest of your staff is aware of what plays and when those plays will be called. By knowing ahead of time what to expect and when to expect it, your staff can be much more effective in watching for key elements of a defense leading up to a call. For example, if you have planned a number of draws in the opening sequence based on the upfield rush of the defense and you have informed your assistants of your plans, they can more effectively watch your opponent and see if indeed the defense is "getting up the field" to the degree you anticipated. There is nothing more frustrating than a coach "after the fact" saying, "I didn't think that was going to work because of the way they were rushing." If your assistants are aware that a draw is coming, they can suggest alternative plays if the defense is not giving you what you expect or want.

Gives the players, especially the quarterback, an excellent chance to get into a rhythm, since they are able to anticipate the next call.

When an offense is in "rhythm", a certain offensive pacing exists in the huddle as well as at the line of scrimmage. When players have practiced a certain sequence of plays, they tend to derive a great deal of confidence from having experienced this sequencing. Ultimately, that confidence should show up in their execution of the game plan. If you can maintain a rhythm, it also puts a great deal of pressure on a defensive coordinator to come up with something that will stop your momentum. As a result, he may be put in a situation where he makes a desperate call and puts his team in a position to give up an "explosive" play.

Allows you to script specific "special" plays and increases your chances of actually getting them run.

Most teams will have a couple of "special" plays as part of their game plan. This could be a new route combination or some type of reverse. Often times, these plays are worked on in practice but are not called in the game because they are not a basic part of your mental-calling sequence. By scripting them in as a part of your openers, you have a much greater chance of actually using them in the game. Furthermore, you can control the specific situation in which you are looking to use them.

If your "openers" are successful, it will give your offense a tremendous amount of confidence.

Naturally, when an offense scores, a certain level of confidence is generated. That confidence is multiplied ten-fold when that scoring sequence has been laid out ahead of time in the classroom and on the practice field. In 1995, for example, Minnesota scored on 50% of the Vikings' opening drives.

Provides you with a great deal of versatility and enables your offense to look very multifaceted and diverse to a defense without having to run a large or unruly number of different plays.

It is obviously an advantage to your offense if you can take some of the aggressiveness out of the defense. By scripting the proper sequence of openers, the offense can confuse and cause hesitation in the defense because the defense is forced to adjust to a number of different looks and plays. If done properly, the offense can create this hesitation without using a huge or unmanageable number of plays.

Building an Opening Sequence

Building an opening sequence involves planning and preparation. For example, you might employ the opening ratios that were discussed earlier in this chapter (Table 2-3).

Openers are an excellent way to test the defense to see what the defense's game plan is.

	1ST DOWN	2ND LONG	2ND MED	2ND SHORT
TOTAL PLAYS	20	10	5	1
1ST HALF PLAYS	10	5	3	1
RUNS	5	2	2	1
PASSES	5	3	1	1
DROP BACK	2	2		
QUICKS	1	1		
PLAY ACTION	2		1	1

Table 2-3. Sample opening sequence.

Employing this play ratio, your efforts to establish an opening sequence could begin with two main formations: regular and two tights (Figures 2-6 and 2-7).

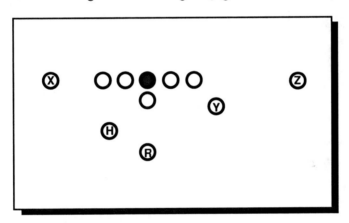

Figure 2-6. Regular—Far RT formation

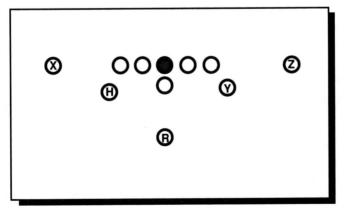

Figure 2-7. Tights-spread formation

Figures 2-8 to 2-17 offer examples of play sequencing off these two basic formations, based on the aforementioned hypothetical opening-play ratio: four dropbacks, two quicks and four play-action passes.

	TIGER (SPREAD)	**REGULAR (FAR-STR MOTION)**
RUNS	• Inside zone	• Weakside iso
	• Trap	• Inside zone
	• Outside zone	• Strongside zone (STR motion)
		• Draw
		• Trap
		• Weakside pitch

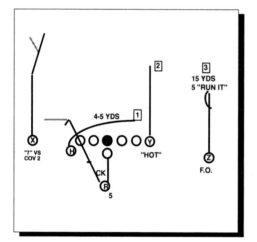

Figure 2-8. Dropback #1.

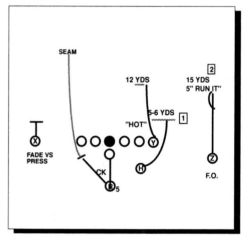

Figure 2-9. Dropback #2.

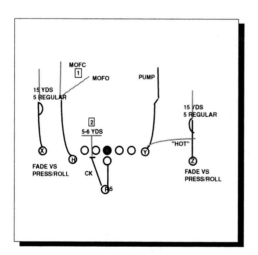

Figure 2-10. Dropback #3.

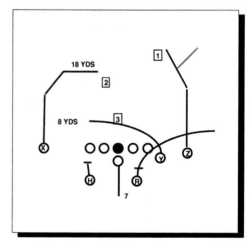

Figure 2-11. Dropback #4.

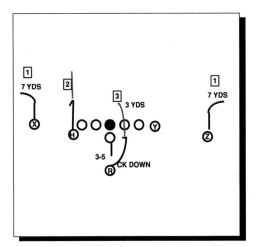

Figure 2-12. Quick #1.

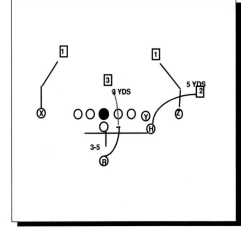

Figure 2-13. Quick #2.

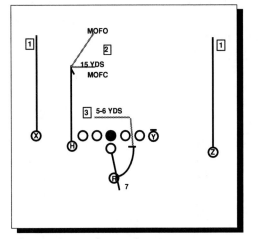

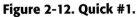

Figure 2-14. Play action #1.

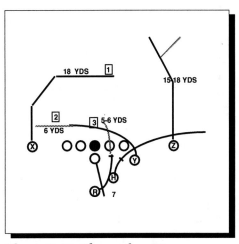

Figure 2-15. Play action #2.

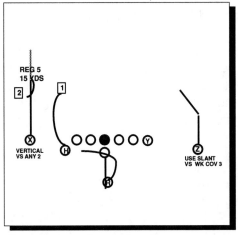

Figure 2-16. Play action #3.

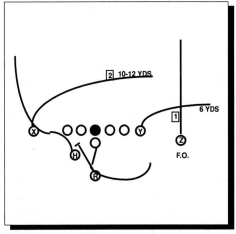

Figure 2-17. Play action #4.

g sequences on first and second down should focus on achieving three
ves:

- Get a first down
- Keep yourself in a convertible third-down distance
- Create an "explosive"

Much of the attention of generating first downs is focused on your third-down package. However, only 25-35% of a team's first downs are generated off third-down conversions. The remaining 65-75% are generated on first and second downs.

In 1994, Minnesota ranked third in the NFL in generating first downs. Of the 325 first downs that the Vikings achieved, 99 came on third downs, while 226 were generated on first and second downs. In 1995, the Vikings earned 342 first downs—114 on third downs, and 228 on first or second downs. Table 2-4 presents earned, first-down conversion figures for six other NFL teams, in addition to Minnesota. These figures show why the third-down conversion, however important, has never been one of the top measurable categories of probability that were discussed earlier in this book.

	EARNED 1ST DOWN	3RD DOWN CONV	%	1ST/2ND CONV	%
MINNESOTA	342	114	33%	228	67%
DENVER	344	89	26%	255	74%
CHICAGO	340	88	26%	252	74%
GREEN BAY	339	108	32%	321	68%
PITTSBURGH	394	97	25%	297	75%
SAN DIEGO	314	95	30%	219	70%
WASHINGTON	297	98	33%	199	67%

Table 2-4. Earned first-down conversion figures for selected NFL teams.

A secondary objective for your first- and second-down calls should be to make sure to leave yourself in as short a third-down situation as possible. As you can see in the third-down section of this book, your chances of conversion on third down nearly doubles from 3rd-and-long to 3rd-and-medium to 3rd-and-short. Accordingly, elements of your play selection should emphasize the +4 yards efficiency on first and second down that was discussed earlier.

One of your final priorities when establishing your opening sequence should be a conscious effort to produce an explosive play. The importance that explosive plays have on the probability of winning, either through scoring or with huge shifts in field position, was documented in an earlier section of this book. Keep in mind that first and second down are the best chances you have for creating explosive plays because of the multiple concerns for which defenses must prepare. If you are creating explosive plays as a basic part of your route progression, or if you have had a couple of broken tackles for big gains, this will suffice. However, if you have gone a couple of series of four, five, or six plays without creating an explosive play, you should create one. In 1995, the Vikings led the NFL in five-minute drives and was second in 10-play drives. Yet, at your best, you are going to only be able to do this less than 20% of the time. The average NFL team had even more difficulty in this area, with teams producing 10-play drives only 11% (22/188) of the time. As Table 2-5 illustrates, the average NFL team in 1995 didn't fare too much better with regard to achieving five-minute drives.

	TOTAL 1ST DOWN	5-MIN. DRIVES	%
MINNESOTA	196	32	16%
CHICAGO	175	27	15%
PITTSBURGH	193	26	13%
SAN DIEGO	177	23	13%
GREEN BAY	180	23	13%
DENVER	181	22	12%
WASHINGTON	185	14	8%

Table 2-5. The ratio of five-minute drives to total number of first-down opportunies for selected NFL teams.

The route combinations in the opening examples cited previously (although a very simplistic approach) show how you might tie your formation and plays together with the aforementioned three priorities in mind. Most of the combinations, given the right defenses, present an opportunity to get a big play down the field or get the first down with some type of underneath route to maintain the +4 yard average.

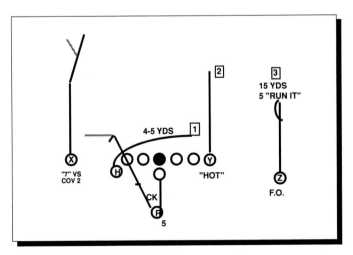

Figure 2-18. Dropback #1 play.

The play illustrated in Figure 2-18 offers a good example of the different priorities you can use in designing your opening sequences. For example, this play gives you a chance to hit X on the skinny post for an "explosion" if you get some form of man-free or three-deep coverage. On the other hand, if the defense rolls its coverage to the weak side, you have a chance to get the first down with the 5 route of the Z receiver. The drop-off routes to the H and R are also high-percentage throws that should maintain your ability to reach your +4 yards efficiency objective.

Summary Points

The key elements in establishing your base offense are:

• Determine the size and scope of the package you need.

• Determine if there is a recognizable difference between first down and second-and-long.

• Establish an opening sequence and be specific with regard to what you want to run and why—then stick by it.

• Keep your opening sequences interactive with regard to personnel and formations.

• Keep your opening priorities in mind:

    ✓ Get a first down
    ✓ Keep yourself in a convertible third-down distance
    ✓ Create an "explosive"

Third Down

As was mentioned in the previous chapter on base offense, the third-down offense is obviously a critical situation. Even though the 25-35% of the first downs generated in this situation are not proportionally as large a part of your total game plan, the significance of maintaining a drive and having three more chances to advance the ball are evident.

As we have done previously, I would like first to examine the scope of the situation. During the four-year period 1992-'95, the average NFL team faced third-down situations between 215-220 times a year. Figure 3-1 illustrates how the distances involved in these circumstances roughly break down:

OVERALL:	AVG	PER
3RD 11+	32	2.0
3RD 7-10	64	4.0
3RD 4-6	48	3.0
3RD 2-3	48	3.0
3RD 1	24	1.5
	216	13.5

Figure 3-1. An average breakdown of third-down situations in the NFL.

These figures can vary depending upon your competitive level. For example, most high school teams are not in the Red Zone as much as college and professional teams. As a result, they don't face as many 3rd-and-longs due to the proportionately lower number of plays that are run. However, the ratios will stay amazingly similar. Figure 3-2 shows an average of how third-down situations are broken down between open field and the Red Zone in the NFL.

The Third-Down Package in the Open Field

The aforementioned numbers reflect the ratios the Vikings faced during the two-year period, 1994-'95 (Figure 3-3). As was mentioned earlier, we encountered a relatively high number of third-down situations due to the nature of our offense and our productivity level on first and second downs.

OPEN FIELD:	AVG	PER
3RD 11+	16	1.0
3RD 7-10	48	3.0
3RD 4-6	32	2.0
3RD 2-3	32	2.0
3RD 1	16	1.0
RED ZONE		
3RD 11+	16	1.0
3RD 7-10	16	1.0
3RD 4-6	16	1.0
3RD 2-3	16	1.0
3RD 1	8	0.5
	216	13.5

Figure 3-2. Third-down situations in the NFL broken down between the open field and the Red Zone.

Open Field:	1994	1995	Avg	Per
3RD 11+	26	30	28	1.75
3RD 7-10	66	55	61	3.78
3RD 4-6	35	46	41	2.53
3RD 2-3	30	20	25	1.56
3RD 1	17	22	20	1.22
Red Zone:				
3RD 11+	4	12	8	0.50
3RD 7-10	28	15	22	1.34
3RD 4-6	5	16	11	0.66
3RD 2-3	16	14	15	0.94
3RD 1	8	11	10	0.59
	235	241	238	15

Figure 3-3. A breakdown of third-down situations faced by the Minnesota Vikings 1994-'95.

This section of the book focuses on the third-down package in the open field. How to prepare fo the third downs that occur in the Red Zone is discussed in Chapter 5. Despite its critical nature, I find this part of the game plan to be one of the easiest to prepare for because the amount of offense needed is so specific and identifiable.

My positive feelings toward dealing with third-down situations are perhaps best reflected by the fact that the Vikings' third-down package was very successful during 1994-'95. In fact, no team in the NFL converted more third downs those two seasons. Furthermore, the Vikings' 47.7% conversion rate in 1995 was the fifth highest conversion rate in the NFL for the previous five years. The Vikings' third-down conversion numbers during the period 1992-'95 are shown in Figure 3-4:

THIRD- DOWN CONVERSIONS					
OPEN FIELD:	1992	1993	1994	1995	AVG
3RD 1					
ATT.	27	16	17	22	21
MADE	16	10	11	20	14
%	59%	63%	65%	91%	70%
3RD 2-3					
ATT.	30	26	33	20	27
MADE	18	13	18	15	16
%	60%	50%	55%	75%	59%
3RD 4-6					
ATT.	42	33	35	46	39
MADE	20	16	13	24	18
%	48%	48%	37%	52%	47%
3RD 7-10					
ATT.	51	48	66	55	55
MADE	11	11	27	13	16
%	22%	23%	41%	24%	28%
3RD 11+					
ATT.	24	33	26	30	28
MADE	3	5	4	8	5
%	13%	15%	15%	27%	18%
TOTAL ATT.	174	156	177	173	170
TOTAL MADE	68	55	73	80	69
TOTAL %	39%	35%	41%	46%	41%

Figure 3-4. The third-down conversion statistics for the Minnesota Vikings during 1992-'95.

The average team in the NFL converts approximately 38-40% of its third-down attempts. In 1995, the highest conversion rate in the NFL was 50% by the Green Bay Packers. Keep in mind that the percentage of success on third-down situations increases substantially as the distance decreases:

- 3rd-and-long   20-25%
- 3rd-and-medium   45-50%
- 3rd-and-short   75-85%

These percentages underline the importance of maintaining a 1st/2nd +4 efficiency. Achieving this level of efficiency enhances your chances of keeping your third-down calls in at least the 50%+ range.

Third-and-Long

Third-and-long is a situation involving any distance greater than +7 yards. By virtue of the distance needed, this area is obviously the most difficult situation to convert. There are two basic approaches you can take in this down-and-distance situation: go for the total distance with a throw down the field; or drop or hand the ball off underneath and give a player a chance to get the distance needed in the open field.

Although the effect of being comfortable with a third-and-7 to 10 or a third-and-11+ situation may involve facing and reacting to a different defense, it usually just involves an adjustment like deepening the depths of some of your individual routes due to the extra distance required for a first down. We usually script five passes for a third-and-long situation, not including whatever base draws or traps we have scheduled for nickel runs. We also always have some form of screen in this situation that is not part of the scripted five passes.

Most defensive teams tend to do one of two things in a long-distance situation: they will either play whatever form of passive zone package they have, emphasizing the importance of keeping the ball in front of them and driving on the underneath route; or they will pressure you, hoping to force a break-off route or a dump pass to a "hot" back, that even if completed, usually falls short of the distance needed for the first down. Of the two scenarios, the former is the most dangerous for the offense. One of the hardest things to do is to get a quarterback to not force the ball into a loaded zone in hopes of making a big play. Knowing when and where to take a chance, and when to drop the ball off and play the percentages is the surest sign of measuring a quarterback's maturity. This factor is the ultimate test of how far the "umbilical cord" between you and the quarterback can stretch. As a coach, you have to understand and keep in mind that coaching can take the player only so far. At some point, either he is capable of making the right decision and executing the play or he isn't.

As a coach, all you can do is lay out and practice the anticipated coverages you will see and make sure the quarterback knows when the percentages are on his side or not. As was discussed earlier, if you provide as much information as you can to the quarterback, you can reduce his level of "uncertainty." In this regard, one of the keys is to educate the quarterback and the team that a one-in four conversion rate in long-yardage situation (7+) is a very successful ratio. A two-in-five conversion rate will put you even further ahead of the curve.

Screens and draws can occasionally catch a defense off guard. Such a scenario, however, is difficult to accomplish with any real consistency. Screens and draws also present an excellent way to simply get out of a series, punt the ball, and start over.

Certainly, situations exist when discretion is the better part of valor. Something can be said, however, for gaining at least some yardage on third down even though it does not convert. For example, a yardage gain that just doesn't quite get there can still be viewed in a positive manner by the offense and give you something to build on. In addition, it may also give you just enough yardage to affect your field position on the next series. On the other hand, taking a sack, throwing an interception (even if it is 40 yards down the field), or just arbitrarily throwing the ball down the field can have a very strong negative effect on the mental state of your team—particularly your offense.

Scripted Passes in a Third-and-Long Situation

Each of the five passes you have scripted for a third-and-long situation should have clearly defined objectives that do one or more of the following:

- Given the right rotation by the secondary, presents you with an opporunity for a deep throw down the field for a substantial gain.

- If given the right one-on-one match up, allows your receiver to run a good route whereby the catch should, at a minimum, gain the yards needed for the first down.

- Provides the quarterback, by way of a dump-off to a primary receiver, with a receiver who has a chance to make an easy catch (preferably facing the defense), allowing him to try to make a move that will enable him to gain the distance needed after the catch.

In the progression shown in the play illustrated in Diagram 3-1, the potential exists for a deep throw down the middle of the field should the defense decide to play a flat "0" coverage with no free safety in the middle of the field, or perhaps a "$^1/_4$-$^1/_4$" halves coverage where the $^1/_4$ strong safety gets pulled up by the inside route of the Y receiver. If the defense sits in a loose cover 2, there is an opportunity to find a window to the inside route by the Y receivers, hopefully at the first-down depth.

If the defense sits in a form of three-deep or man-free, you may have a chance to work the backside 5 route if you like the match up with your X receiver and the left cornerback. If you are going to use this route in third-and-long situations, you may want to deepen the depth of the 5 route to 18 yards. If the quarterback is forced to dump the ball to the swing receiver (R), at least the running back is moving down the field and may have the chance to make a move and get the first down.

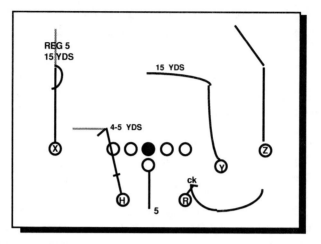

Diagram 3-1.

Forcing a "hot" throw or "break off" can be an effective tactic by the defense—but one that carries great risk. If a defensive team attempts this, it will usually be done in one of two ways: a zone dog/blitz with pressure coming from one side or the other, accompanied by zone coverage behind it; a more aggressive dog/blitz with increased pressure, possibly from both sides, and man coverage behind it. This scenario is a situation where your quarterback must have a thorough knowledge of his protection schemes. If it is a zone dog/blitz, and the defense has not brought sufficient people from the correct side to pressure him, the quarterback should not panic and force the ball too quickly if he indeed has adequate protection to pick up the pressure. On the other hand, if the defensive pressure exposes the quarterback to a free rusher, he must be fully aware of his vulnerability and must have been schooled on what his options are at that point.

A four-man, weakside dog is a typical situation that the quarterback must be ready to face. Diagram 3-2 illustrates protection #1—a seven-player, man-based protection scheme that the offense should have no difficulty picking up the fourth defender from the weakside. Diagram 3-3 depicts protection #2—a six-player, man-based scheme with the center committed to the strongside. If you are not able to redirect the center to the four-man side, the quarterback must be prepared to hit a "hot" or "break off" receiver if both the linebackers come.

Few defensive teams do this type of blitzing arbitrarily. If a team has a history of zone dog/blitz or total pressure, you must make sure your quarterback is aware of his options with every route that is installed. Again, you should remember that an effective "hot" or "break off" route, even if it doesn't achieve the first down, is far preferable to the quarterback getting sacked and maybe even fumbling.

A run in a third-and-long, down-and-distance situation is worth a shot particularly if you keep the one-in-four ratio in mind and have already converted at least on one third-

and-long play. The NFL average for runs in this situation is only 11 per team a year, converting on two. The team with the most 3rd-and-7+ run conversions in 1995 was Jacksonville with seven conversions in 17 attempts.

One additional point concerning this situation should be considered. I often see teams making a deep-play fake to an "I" back in a third-and-long. I understand that some teams may only have a certain route combination tied to a particular protection scheme, usually some form of a turnback zone. If you are not willing to carry an additional protection and drop the quarterback straight back, you should at least school the quarterback to take a drop with the turnback protection that allows him to abandon the fake in this situation. While I understand play-action fakes can be helpful, in this down-and-distance situation, I doubt you are going to fool anyone. As a result, you should never make the quarterback take his eyes off coverage rotation unless a play fake is going to substantially help the route.

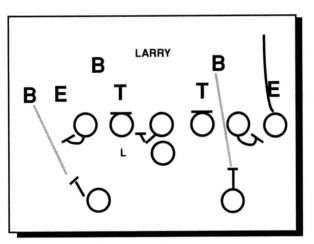

Diagram 3-2. Protection #1.

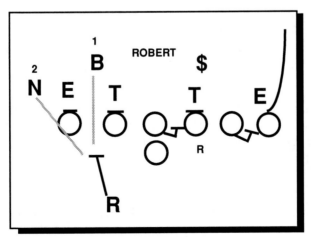

Diagram 3-3. Protection #2.

3rd-and-Medium

A third-and-medium situation involves both the "third-and-two to three yards" and the "third-and-four to six yards" packages. Both scenarios involve separate and distinct packages. The major difference between the two situations lies in the ability of a run to get the yardage needed. We usually carry a total of six plays in third-and-medium, four plays in third-and-four to six yards, and two plays in third-and-two to three yards.

Conversions on third-and-medium are absolutely critical because of the effect they can have on your play-calling mentality. If you are confident and successful in this situation, your first- and second-down calls can take on a whole additional dimension when you know that you can convert a majority of your third-and-mediums. Accordingly, this capability may allow you to take more chances at verticals on first down knowing that all you have to do with your second-down call is get to a third-and-medium, or you may be willing to do more with your second-and-medium plays knowing you are already in a high-percentage, third-down situation. On the other hand, if your third-and-medium offense does not have a substantially higher success ratio than your third-and-long offense, you are less apt to stay with the run in a second-and-long situation. As a result, you may lose much of the balance that most teams strive to achieve.

In a "third-and-four to six" situation, a run other than a draw or a trap is relatively hard to consistently get the full 4-6 yards. Keep in mind that even the best of running teams in the NFL during the period 1992-'95 averaged just one run a game in "third-and-anything over two yards" situations. Even with this in mind, it is always one of my goals to get at least one run a game in a true third-down, medium-to-long situation.

Play-action passes become legitimate fakes in a third-down, medium-distance situation, particularly as the distance needed decreases. It is important that you use play fakes that are tied to runs. Our runs in this situation are most always draws or traps, so our play-action series consists of fake draws or fake-trap series.

A third-and-medium situation is also a scenario where special care should be taken to match the plays up by formation and personnel. We often use a series of shifts and motions on two or three of the plays with very different routes on each play. Also, we prefer not to run plays at this point that have been used earlier in the game. If we are using a base combination that we use a lot on a first and second down, we wait until we have used it in this situation before we go back to using it in a normal, down-and-distance situation.

Diagrams 3-4 to 3-6 illustrate the play progression of some route combinations that are run by many teams in the NFL. We usually include a quick hitch out in this situation, either as a primary or a backside route. Many times, this simple and efficient play can get the desired results.

3rd-and-Short

The most important thing to remember in a 3rd-and-1 situation is that you are usually in this situation only once a game. Your limited exposure to third-and-short certainly doesn't

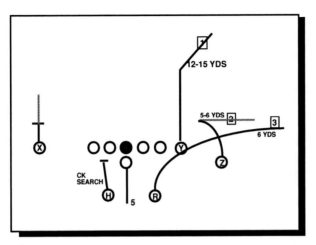

Diagram 3-4.

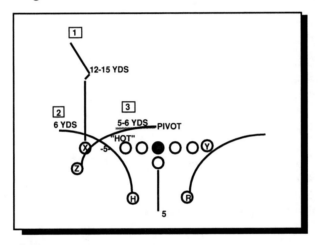

Diagram 3-5.

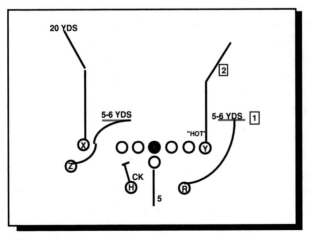

Diagram 3-6.

mean that you should only carry one play in your game plan to deal with it. On the other hand, some coaches often include as many as eight to nine plays in their offensive game plan for this situation.

Two basic trains of thought exist regarding this down-and-distance situation: get the first down, or take a shot at a big play. The conversion rate for a third-and-short situation is not as high as you might think. The average conversion rate of the NFL during the four-year period, 1992-'95, was around 65-70%. In 1995, for example, the Minnesota Vikings led the NFL in third-and-1 conversions by converting 30 of 36 attempts (83 %). That figure jumped to 91% percent in the open field.

In 1995, the Vikings' run/pass ratio in a third-and-short situation looked like this:

20 of 23 runs
10 of 13 passes

The Vikings' basic approach on third-and-short situations was to run the ball from three separate personnel groupings each game. We carried a three-tight end (Jumbo), smash-ball play, and a normal two-back or two-tights play, and we spread the defense with a 3- or 4-wide personnel formation. As a point of fact, during the period 1993-'95, the NFL teams that had the highest conversion rate on third-and-short situations used just a quarterback wedge to gain a first down on numerous occasions.

Occasionally, a defensive team will cover off your center and both guards and even pepper (i.e., step-up into the gap) one or more linebackers into the gaps. For this purpose, you must have an audible ready to take advantage of the other vulnerabilities a defense that commits to this type of alignment will present to you.

If you decide to carry a play with "big play" or touchdown potential, you should be certain that it is just that—a big play. You would hate to take the chance of passing up a high-percentage third-and-1 run for a "big play" that only gets 5-10 yards. A jumbo formation is probably the best formation with which to break a big play. A play-action fake over your best blockers with your best back, particularly in a critical situation, is your best chance of bringing the secondary up into the position you want. Keep in mind that you are usually only going to be in this situation once a game. As such, you may practice this "big" play every week for six weeks and never use it. However, the repetitions you put into this play may pay big dividends when you need them the most.

Given the nature of your level of play, you may find you are in more third- or fourth-and-1 situations. For example, because of your lack of a kicking game, you may find yourself in more four-down situations where you are willing to go for it more on a fourth-and-1 situation than might otherwise be typically seen on the professional level. As with any situation, you should determine what you will probably need to win the game and how committed you are to going for it. These are decisions that should be made during the week, rather than during the "heat of battle" on game day.

Summary Points

The key elements in establishing your third-down package are:

- Determine the size and scope of your package.

- Recognize the success ratio you can expect in each phase:

✓	3rd and Long	20-25%
✓	3rd and Medium	45-50%
✓	3rd and Short	75-85%

- Leave your options open for your quarterback and be certain that he understands what his options are.

- Have a plan to handle the blitz.

- Match your plays by personnel and formation.

- Determine your plan for a third-and-short situation during the week and stay with your plan.

CHAPTER 4

Pre-Red Zone

No one could logically question the fact that efficiency in the Red Zone is vitally important to winning any game. However, an area many game plans don't adequately account for is the part of the field leading up to the Red Zone. A pre-Red Zone offense is particularly important if you have a field goal kicker who has an effective range from at least 20 to 30 yards. When I was with the Vikings, we were very fortunate to have Fuad Reveiz as our field goal kicker. Fuad was extremely accurate from the 30-yard line in. As evidence of his accuracy, at one time, Fuad held the NFL record with 30 consecutive field goals.

Given Fuad's exceptional skills, coupled with the importance of Red Zone efficiency, we established the pre-Red Zone area as a critical area of our situational game plan. We knew that once we got past the 30-yard line, we had a very high degree of success in getting at least three points.

The priority for us once we crossed the 50-yard line was to employ a combination of plays that increased our chances of crossing the 30-yard line. We accomplished this goal in two ways: utilizing plays that have the highest degree of success in the 10-15-yard range; and though you do not want to become too conservative in your approach, avoiding plays that might put your team in a position where they have to convert a third-and-long just to get into scoring position. To accomplish this, we took special care not to run plays that had the potential for a big loss (reverses or sweeps) or protections that had the quarterback sitting deep in the pocket, making a lot of reads.

The pre-Red-Zone is an excellent place on the field to run your quick passing game or rollouts by the quarterback. If you do not have a kicker with the type of consistency that we had with Fuad, your pre-Red Zone approach may take on a whole different perspective. The closer you get to the Red Zone, the harder it becomes to just physically overwhelm your opponent and push the ball in for the score. Likewise, the passing lanes become tighter and tighter with every yard as you approach the end zone. For this reason, you may need to use the pre-Red Zone area as a place to take a high number of vertical shots. It is also a area where you may want to run your specials. In both instances, whether you are simply focusing on getting the ball inside the 30-yard line or taking extra vertical shots, you should establish a three- or four-play progression covering the objectives you set for your team.

It is important that you make your team aware of the priorities you have established for the pre-Red-Zone area so that your quarterback knows what is expected of him in this situation, and how many risks he may want or need to take. Based on your team's kicking capabilities, this situation is also a scenario where you should determine how far out you will extend your fourth-down territory. This factor is something that should be planned for during the week and explained to your players prior to the game. If you go for a fourth down and have not made your team aware of your intentions to do so earlier, they may misinterpret your actions as evidence of panic on your part.

CHAPTER 5

Red Zone

Along with converting third downs, the Red Zone is clearly the most critical situation the offense will be in during the course of a game. Like third down, the size and scope of the Red Zone can be very specifically defined. This area is actually divided into three distinct areas: Red Zone, +10 yards, and goal line.

During the four-year period, 1992-'95, the average team in the NFL had 45-50 series a season in the Red Zone and converted its Red Zone possessions to points between 80-85% of the time. This averaged out to about three Red Zone possessions a game. Table 5-1 illustrates how often selected NFL teams found themselves in the Red Zone during that period.

RED ZONE:	MINN	DENVER	CHICAGO	GREEN BAY	PITTS	SAN DIEGO	WASH	TEAM AVG	PER GAME AVG
1ST DOWN	78	63	79	74	75	63	74	72	4.5
2ND LONG	50	37	43	44	51	43	57	45	2.8
2ND MED	45	35	48	31	40	23	30	36	2.3
2ND 1	7	10	7	6	10	7	6	8	0.5
3RD 11+	12	3	1	1	9	12	7	6	0.4
3RD 7-10	15	16	19	17	24	16	19	18	1.1
3RD 4-6	16	17	24	13	18	8	18	16	1.0
3RD 2-3	14	9	6	19	8	15	17	13	0.8
3RD 1	11	11	10	7	5	4	5	8	0.5
4TH	7	6	9	3	16	6	10	8	0.5
1ST GOAL	24	28	45	30	35	23	25	30	1.9
									16.3

Table 5-1. A breakdown of Red Zone situations for selected NFL teams.

During 1994-'95, for example, the Minnesota Vikings had 54 and 57 Red Zone possessions, respectively. Table 5-2 depicts how the Vikings' Red Zone down-and-distance distribution looked during the period 1992-'95.

Previously, the importance of Red Zone efficiency and how it was one of the top four in measurable probability with respect to winning a game was discussed. The Vikings' contrast in Red Zone efficiency from 1993 to 1994 was a case study in the importance of Red Zone efficiency. Earlier in the book, the limitations on our offense in 1993 compared to our production in 1994 when we set the all-time total offensive yardage mark were delineated. In 1993, the Vikings had 45 Red Zone possessions and scored 43 times for a 96% conversion rate. That percentage led the league in that season. In 1994, on the other hand, the Vikings were a good deal more productive and had 54 Red Zone possessions but had only 44 scores, falling back to the NFL average of 80%. Had we maintained our 90%+ efficiency rating in 1994, we would have scored 400+ points. During the 1995 season, the Vikings' Red Zone efficiency improved to the point where we broke the Minnesota Vikings' all-time seasonal scoring record for 412 points.

RED ZONE:	1992	1993	1994	1995	AVG	Game AVG
1ST SERIES	9	7	4	12	8	0.50
1ST 10+	2	1	4	3	3	0.16
1ST EARNED	60	51	70	63	61	3.81
1ST GOAL	25	26	20	24	24	1.48
2ND LONG	41	44	52	50	47	2.92
2ND MED	26	27	29	45	32	1.98
2ND 1	13	8	6	7	9	0.53
3RD 11+	7	3	4	12	7	0.41
3RD 7-10	10	18	28	15	18	1.11
3RD 4-6	11	17	5	16	12	0.77
3RD 2-3	13	10	16	14	13	0.83
3RD 1	10	9	8	11	10	0.59
4TH	4	1	9	7	5	0.33

Table 5-2. A breakdown of Red Zone down-and-distance situations for the Minnesota Vikings, 1992-'95.

Given these parameters, we have approximately 10 plays (five runs and five passes) for first and second down in the Red Zone. We also have two plays for third-and-long and third-and-medium. Typically, we carry our third-and-1 play over from our open-field package. We also carry three or four end-zone plays that are prioritized by field position (+25 to +15; +15 to +10; +10 to +5).

More and more teams are playing a loose four-across zone concept inside the Red Zone. The result is that there are fewer of the man-for-man match ups that made pick routes very prominent in years past. This zone concept puts a higher priority on being able to run the ball effectively and hitting underneath routes that (hopefully) enable receivers to score after catching the ball. Three of the top four teams in touchdown efficiency in the NFL in 1995 were Philadelphia, Dallas and Seattle—not surprisingly, teams that were also three of the top rushing teams in the NFL that season.

Previously, mention was made about the pre-Red Zone area and the priority of getting into scoring position. Whatever the range of your field goal kicker, it is important that once you get inside that range, you minimize the chance of being pushed back out of that area. Accordingly, once we cross the 30-yard line, we are very careful to not run plays that carry the potential for a loss that would take us out of field-goal range. This means avoiding calling deep-drop routes or special plays that could result in losing yards out of this area. Once we cross the 20-yard line, however, we are less concerned with the depth of our drops causing a sack that might keep us out of field-goal range.

Defenses tend to begin their Red Zone defensive packages at different places from the +20 to the +10. Teams tend to be very specific about what they will run vs. different personnel groupings. Lawyers have a saying, "Don't ask a question you don't already know the answer to". This advice is very valuable. In other words, be very hesitant to introduce a personnel or formation grouping to which you don't have a pretty good idea of how the defense is going to react. This situation is no place to surprise your quarterback. The Red Zone is also an excellent place for different plays from formations you may have run in the open field. This approach may cause hesitation in a defense when it thinks that it has seen something before, and you run counter to that.

+10

In 1995, the average team in the NFL had 26 first-and-goal-to-go series. The better teams in the league will usually have between 35-40 series in this area of the field. In either case, you should plan for about two series a game involving this situation. The size of the amount of offense we may need to deal with this specific situation each week suggests that you should have a specific plan for your two or three runs in this area, and should base one or two passes off of those formations.

This close to the goal line, because every pass is virtually a shot for the end zone, the quarterback must be very focused on what he expects to see before he throws the ball. Because this is an area in which it is very hard to account for everyone, the quarterback is more vulnerable to being intercepted. Nothing tends to demoralize an offense more than to move the ball the length of the field, than to turn the ball over so close to scoring.

Goal Line

Like your short-yardage offense, the goal line is an area for which it is easy to carry too much offense into the game plan. In 1995, the average NFL team ran three plays a game in a goal-line situation. Table 5-3 illustrates the Vikings' ration over the four-year period, 1992-'95.

	1992	1993	1994	1995	Yearly AVG	Game AVG
GOAL LINE	34	35	41	36	37	2.3

Table 5-3. The number of goalline plays run by the Minnesota Vikings, 1992-'95.

You should be aware of the fact that you will rarely run more than three or four goal-line plays during the course of a game. As a result, you will seldom need more than three runs and one play action off your primary formation to deal with this particular situation. Keep in mind that you can always use one of your +10 plays or one of your 2-point plays on the goal line.

Two-Point Plays

With its adoption of the two-point rule, the NFL is in alignment with high school and college play sequencing. With regard to two-point plays, however, there are two major differences in the NFL:

- The NFL's two-point line is at the two-yard line, making the run much more viable.

- With the possibility of overtime, the use of two-point plays, particularly at the end of a game, appears to be somewhat of a less critical factor in the NFL. While the NCAA changed the Division 1A rule to allow for overtime, the NFL (due to its conservative nature) is less likely to go for two points and the win late in the game, than one point and take its chances in overtime.

In 1995, most NFL teams averaged only one two-point play a year, with the highest number being the five attempts by the Arizona Cardinals. This statistic was down from the previous year, when the NFL averaged two 2-point attempts a year.

We normally carry three 2-point plays into most games. While this number is extremely high given the number of 2-point plays actually run, we pointed out earlier that it is also a reasonsable way to expand your goal line offense. As a result, our efforts involving two-point plays have a lot of carryover value. Most of our 2-point plays are run out of our regular and the three-wides personnel alignments. As a result, this setup can also serve as a contrast of choices to your normal goal line offense that utilizes three tight ends.

Regarding two-point plays, one of the major coaching points for your quarterback is to remember that an interception can not be returned for any points on two-point attempts. For this reason, he should go down fighting and if all else appears lost, just throw the ball up for grabs if there is no clear place to go. This situation certainly differs from a third-down attempt made from the same area, where the option of kicking a field goal is still available, or if it is fourth-down, a "lost" ball can be returned by the defense for points. This rule differs in the college game where the defense can return a 2-point conversion for an equal number of points.

Summary Points

The key elements in establishing your Red Zone package are:

- Determine the size and scope of your Red Zone package.

- Determine the abilities of your kicking game, and once inside field-goal range, never put yourself in position to be taken out of that range.

- Eliminate as many "surprises" in your offensive plan for the Red Zone as you can; this area involves a situation where you must have the most detailed part of your game plan.

- Coordinate your +10, goal line, and 2-point plan to be interactive. Be prepared to carry one aspect of your plan into the other.

CHAPTER 6

Special Categories

This section of the book examines the special categories that do not take up a substantial percentage of your game plan. In some instances, these situations may not even come up in a game. When they do occur, however, they can be critical to the outcome of a game. These special category areas include:

- Backed-up offense
- Special first-down plays
- Blitz situations
- Two-minute offense
- Four-minute offense
- Last three plays of the game/half

Backed-Up Offense

Teams in the NFL are not normally backed up on their goal line as much as high school or college teams are. Regardless of the level at which you are coaching, however, you should have an adequate offensive package ready for this situation. We basically prepare one offensive series for our backed-up offensive needs.

The primary objective for a backed-up situation is obvious: get at least one first down. At this point, the opponent's goal line looks a million miles away and the offense may feel a little pressured. It is important, however, to keep the focus of the offensive team on the most immediate task at hand. For example, the intermediate goal of getting one first down will allow them to focus on a much less imposing chore.

If the ball is literally backed up to the goal line, your linemen must be even more aware of their splits, and the players handling the ball must take extra care. We carry two base plays in this situation and an additional third-and-medium and third-and-long call. These plays are base calls with which we are very familiar and in which the players have a great deal of confidence. Although they are base plays, that does not mean they have to be the most conservative plays in the playbook.

Bobby Bowden, the extremely successful coach at Florida State, gave a clinic speech on backed-up offense aptly named, "Hang loose, one of us is fixing to score!" This approach is an excellent one to take in this situation. If you are unable to get the first down and get out from under the shadow of your goal post, the chances are very good that your opponent will convert this opportunity into some form of points.

If you are willing to throw the ball in this situation, you have a relatively good chance to hit something down the field, since most defenses tend to play fairly conservatively in this situation. It is important that your quarterback knows what is expected of him in this situation and what he should do based on the expected fronts and coverages. Keep in mind that this situation can turn into a real positive for your offense. It can be very demoralizing for a defense when they let an offense out of this situation. If you are able to get a first down, your next play is an excellent time to take a shot down the field.

Special First-Down Plays

This part of your special categories covers two plays: "first down-and-less-than-10" and "first-down-and-more-than-10." The first-and-less-than-10 situation is usually a first-and-5 due to an offsides penalty called on the defense. Most teams in the NFL face this situation only a few times a year. Frankly, I don't imagine it happens much more at either the high school or collegiate levels. Still, you want to be prepared with a call. Many people use this situation as a chance to take a shot at a big play, figuring they are already at second-and-medium at worst. The only problem with this philosophy is the defense is usually thinking the same thing and is probably in a mode that can make a big play even harder to successfully complete.

What you can do in this situation is to run a play that sets up a big play down the road, or call a play that runs counter to something you use a lot or have already run. Although getting a true "explosive" may be harder to accomplish, a good solid 10-yard gain is always welcome yardage. Of course, taking advantage of the situation to just pound out another first down is not the worst play call either.

First-and-10+ unfortunately happens with much more frequency during a game and is something that must be a part of every game plan. This situation occurs, on the average, once a game—much more frequently than does first-and-less-than-10.

The key to this situation is to recognize that a legitimate priority is to just get back to second-and-10 or better. Third-and-11+ is the longest odds you will face in any situation in football and should be avoided at all cost. It is no surprise that the NFL teams who have faced the most third-and-11+ situations a year are the same teams with the worst third-down conversion rates.

With this in mind, you should school your team to understand the importance of getting back to a respectable second-down distance. You can help your team by properly analyzing what the defense will probably do in a first-and-more-than-10 situation. Such a situation usually comes up after an illegal procedure call or a holding call on the offense. In your weekly preparation, it is important to analyze if a defense has a pattern to what it does in either a first-and-less-than-10 or a first-and-more-than-10 situation, and if each situation elicits a separate tendency by the defense.

This distance is one of those situations that, numerically, is so small it is easy to package and prepare your team to face. Like all offensive situations, if you can accurately predict what the defense will do in this very specific circumstance, your team should have a great deal of confidence knowing the play that they are running is designed for this specific situation. The play you call in this instance certainly does not have to be a special play or anything you don't normally run. On the contrary, it should be something your team is very comfortable wit h and has experienced a reasonable amount of success using.

Blitz Situations

In 1994 and 1995, teams in the NFL faced a true blitz situation a little over a 100 times a year. This total averaged out to about 6-7 blitzes per game per team. The NFL keeps track of how each team does by assigning percentages to attempts vs. completions, yards gained, touchdowns or turnovers, and sack ratio. By assigning these totals a rating (much like the quarterback rating the league uses to make their quarterback rankings), the NFL ranks each team on its ability to handle the blitz. Table 6-1 illustrates how seven NFL teams handled the blitz (comparatively speaking) in 1995. Minnesotas' 108.97 rating led the NFL that season. In 1994, the Vikings' ranked sixth in the league with an 89.9 rating.

	ATT	COMP	YDS	TD	T.O.	SACKS	RATING
MINNESOTA	141	87	1097	11	1	10	108.97
GREEN BAY	112	66	1019	7	3	11	98.77
DENVER	92	42	646	9	3	7	93.84
CHICAGO	127	74	567	4	2	1	88.3
PITTSBURGH	115	65	866	4	3	7	80.56
SAN DIEGO	107	49	582	6	6	7	58.24
WASHINGTON	94	39	432	3	4	15	48.71

Table 6-1. How select NFL teams handled the blitz in 1995.

We usually carry two or three "blitz beaters" in our game plan. -These are specific plays (protections) that can be called or audibled to take advantage of specific pressure defenses. Most pressure fronts can be handled with your basic plays by hitting a hot route or in some instances by redirecting the run. If there is a specific pressure package you are worried about, or if there is one that you think presents an opportunity to hit a big play, this situation is the instance you are looking for to use one of your "blitz beaters". A blitz beater could be something as simple as a quick slant or a more elaborate as an eight-man protection scheme with a throw down the field. In either case, it is important that your team know what your objective is in using this play and when you expect to go to it.

This part of your game plan is one that mentally and emotionally must be addressed with your team. We have always taken the approach that the blitz is an "opportunity" rather than something that should be feared. We stress that a blitz is a chance to make a big play or create one of the "explosives" we are consistently trying to run.

You should be careful about relying on an eight-man protection scheme as the basis of your blitz beaters. Often, this scheme is something that a team may spend a great deal of time on and yet only use a few times a year. If an eight-man protection scheme is only something that you audible to in extreme situations, it probably is not a procedure that you are going to execute with a great deal of confidence.

On the other hand, if you can put a viable package together to deal with a blitz situation that is more a part of your base offense and is something you do on a more regular basis, it will increase your chances of success a great deal. Keep in mind that if a team is committed to the blitz, like former Arizona Cardinals' coach Buddy Ryan's package, then you must obviously expand your blitz package. In fact, you should make it the basis of your game plan that week.

Two-Minute Offense

The two-minute offense is a very challenging, yet exciting, part of any game. It is an area of the offense that must be practiced each week. Furthermore, your two-minute offense should have a very specific structure with regard to procedures and plays. Every player, not just the quarterback, should be aware of the rules that affect any two-minute situation, most importantly what affects the game clock. A multitude of "clock" situations exist that could affect this period. Nothing looks worse than to see a team staring at each other during this time period, wondering whether they should huddle or use a no-huddle offense. It is difficult to make your players aware of every situation. We subscribe to the following general rule:

| WHAT STOPS THE CLOCK-STARTS THE CLOCK! |

What this rule encompasses is the concept that if the officials stop the play, then the officials will spot the ball and play will resume immediately. On the other hand, if the ball stops the play (incomplete pass or the player running out of bounds), then it takes the next snap of the ball to start the clock and you have time to huddle.

Most offenses have a no-huddle offense for this part of their game plan. In addition, it is a good time to have and practice a two-play sequence, (i.e., calling two plays in the huddle). Such a sequence is particularly useful inside the Red Zone.

"Killing" the clock by the spiking of the ball can also be an effective tool if you have few or no time-outs. In a few situations, for example—after a long gain and if time requires it, spiking the ball on first down is sometimes preferable to rushing a play and being forced into a couple of critical calls that have to be made at the line.

Above all else, the quarterback, and if possible the team, must be schooled as to what your objective is (touchdown or field goal) in a two-minute offensive situation, what field position is needed if you are positioning for a field goal, and what your time-out situation is. In addition, this is an aspect of the game where you, as the coach, must be able to take as much pressure off the quarterback as possible. A signal system should be used for the quarterback so that he can check with you on every play as to what needs to be done—run, pass or call time out.

Four-Minute Offense

This aspect of the offense is one we all like working with because it indicates we are in control of the game and are trying to run the clock out. Like the two-minute offense, it is vital that your quarterback and team know exactly what is expected during the four-minute offense, what the rules are, and what plays they can anticipate being run.

One of the more common phrases used in football is, "a running clock is worth 35 seconds." Your team should remember that getting a first down is the second priority in this situation to the number one priority of keeping the clock running.

You should school your offense about what personnel and formation groupings will be used in the four-minute offense, especially if they are groupings that you do not use regularly or have not planned to use a lot in this game. The last thing you want to do is stop the clock because you don't have the right people on the field. Furthermore, it is best that you limit your passing offense to action passes that break containment, and that the quarterback knows that incompletions are not an option in this situation. A sack and loss of yardage is far more preferable to stopping the clock.

You should carry a number of baserunning plays from appropriate formations that can be used during your four-minute offense. These are all usually plays that are a base part of the game plan or plays that you run every week and plays that the players are familiar with without a lot of extra practice. If you are going to spend time in practice on your four-minute offense, you should focus on the passes you may want to use in this situation. This step will help school your quarterback in the different priorities of passing the ball in this situation.

Last Three Plays

We carry three plays for the end of the half or the end of the game that include the desperation "hail Mary" or special "flea flickers" run down the field. These plays should be practiced every week and should be run regardless of whether the score is 40-0 or 14-10. It should be reemphasized to your players that a game cannot end on a defensive penalty. Furthermore, if a field goal can win the game, your field goal team must be up and ready. This step is something that must be practiced during the week.

A final note that you should consider with regard to this situation and your two-minute offense. It is obviously important that your players do not sense that you are panicked in this situation. Keep in mind that your confidence and poise can carry over to your players. However, this situation is critical with time being a major factor. Your normal demeanor will probably change, no matter how confident and poised you are, simply because time dictates a much more "hurried" pace. School your players about how your demeanor may change so that they do not misinterpret your change in character as a sign of possible panic on your part.

Summary Points

The key elements in establishing your special category package are:

- Determine the size and scope of each package even if it is unlikely it will come up.

- Coach your players to understand the unique properties of each of these situations.

- Stress the importance of preparing for each situation; reinforce the fact that it may come down to one of these situations to win a game.

- Make sure that the players know your intentions in each of these areas and do not misinterpret your actions as a sign of panic.

CHAPTER 7

Installing the Offense

To this point in this text, a good deal of time has been devoted to analyzing the size and scope of each of the situations for which an offense must prepare. Table 7-1 summarizes the amount of offense that has been determined that we need by situation.

		SCRIPT	REPEAT
BACKED UP	BASE		2
	3RD MED		1
	3RD LONG		1
OPEN FIELD	1ST DOWN	30	
	1ST 5		1
	1ST 15		1
	2ND LONG	15	
	2ND MED	7	
	2ND 1		2
	3RD LONG	5	
	3RD 4-5	4	
	3RD 2-3	2	
	3RD 1	3	
	4TH 1		1
RED ZONE	1ST DOWN	6	
	2ND DOWN	4	
	3RD MED	2	
	3RD 1		1
	4TH 1		1
	END ZONE	3	
	+10	4	
	GOAL LINE	3	
	2-POINT	3	
		91	11

Table 7-1. A breakdown of the offense required for a particular situation.

The scripted column represents the upper limit of plays needed for a particular situation, keeping our 25-30% overage factor in mind. The repeat column constitutes plays that will probably come from other parts of the game plan. As such, these plays don't necessarily have to be separately scripted plays. You must, however, make sure these situations are covered and that everyone is aware of what is going to be run.

I am by no means suggesting you have to have 90 different play combinations. Much of what you will call will be repeated or changed subtly by either formation or personnel. The listed 91 plays fall within the 20-25% overage we outlined earlier. As large as this number (91) may seem, many teams will unknowingly carry a much higher percentage of overage, thus making the practice ratio of game-plan to actual-plays-called even higher.

There is a certain comfort zone that all coaches can easily fall into while preparing their team. By simply loading up the game plan with a superfluous number of plays, or by practicing in a manner in which the players simply run through a relatively high number of plays, coaches can fool themselves into thinking they have covered everything they can and it is now up to their players.

Keep in mind that it is also very easy to oversimplify a game plan in the guise of being "fundamentally sound" or not being too "complicated" for the players. According to Bill Walsh, in his previously quoted article, "Some coaches rely on relatively simplistic plans. When their plans don't work, they say that it was the players who did not block hard enough, did not run hard enough, or just were not tough enough."

The point to remember is that the size and complexity of any game plan and the way you install it are not the issue. What is at issue is whether you, as a coach, have taken the time to be as detailed and specific in your game plan preparation as is needed to give your players the best chance to succeed.

Game-Plan Board

To this point, an overview of what parameters should be used to determine what each offensive situation consists of and how much offense is needed in each situation has been provided. We employ a "game-plan board" to assist our coaching staff in this regard.

Diagram 7-1 illustrates how our "game-plan board" is arranged in our offensive coaches' meeting room. We fill this board as we progress through our situational discussions. This system makes it very easy to make changes, compare plays and formations, and, in general, give everyone a reference point from which to check the game plan at any given time.

In the previous discussion on "openers" in this book, the concept of the coaching staff's ability to be on top of both the game plan and the sequencing of the calls as being a major reason for establishing your openers with your coaches was discussed. Using a game-plan board to lay out the game plan is an excellent way to achieve your objectives in this regard.

BASE RUN	BASE PASS	2ND LONG	3RD 11+	PRED RED ZONE	+10
			3RD 7-10	RED ZONE RUN	GOAL
		2ND MED	3RD 4-6	RZ BASE PASS	
			3RD 2-3	RZ END ZONE	BACKED UP: 1ST DOWN: 1. 2.
	PLAY ACTION	VERTICALS			
SCREEN			NICKEL RUNS	PRESSURE/ BLITZ	3RD MED: 3RD LONG:
SPEC. RUN					
	ACTION PASS	2ND - 1	3RD - 1	RED ZONE SY	LAST 3 PLAYS
SPEC. PASS					

Diagram 7-1. Sample game-plan board.

Game-Week Time Line

The following outline illustrates how we break up our week based on a normal Sunday game:

MONDAY

11:00 a.m.	Individual coaches finish viewing and grading game video. View film as an offensive/defensive staff; group viewing and analysis of video.
1:00 p.m.	Staff meeting
2:00	Team meeting
	Special teams viewing
2:30	Video viewing
4:15	On the field (practice)
4:45	Practice ends; the coaches view video independently
6:00	Dinner
	Coaches view game video independently and begin their individual game-lan contributions.

TUESDAY

8:00 a.m.	Offensive staff meets and discusses *base run and protections.*
10:00	Offensive line coaches begin run and protection sheets, and view SY-GL - Red Zone
	Offense staff lists *base pass, play action, and action passes.*
11:30	Lunch , work out, miscellaneous
2:00 p.m.	Offensive staff lists *nickel passes* and *nickel runs.*
4:00	Staff meets to list *SY-GL*
5:00	Staff begins to list *Red Zone*
6:00	Dinner
7:00	Review *blitz*
	Finalize:

      ✓ Script board
      ✓ Scripts and cards
      ✓ Scouting report

WEDNESDAY

7:30 a.m.	Staff meeting
8:15	QB meeting
8:30	Special team meeting
9:00	Team meeting (5)
	Scouting report
	Install base run, nickel runs, and protections
10:00	Offensive line breaks off
	Install base pass, play-action, action passes, nickel passes
10:30	Individual meetings

11:15	Walk through
11:45	Lunch
12:45 p.m.	Individual meetings (flexible)
	View opponent's video
1:15	Meetings over
1:30	Special teams meeting
2:00	Practice
4:15	Practice over
5:15	Coaches review practice video
	Finalize Red Zone offense
	List backed-up and four-Minute
	Review script board and prepare cards for Thursday practice

THURSDAY

7:30 a.m.	Staff meeting
8:15	QB meeting
8:30	Special teams meeting
9:00	Team meeting (5)
	View practice (OL separate)
10:00	Offense together installs SY-GL-Red Zone -backed up
10:30	Individual meeting (view opponent's film)
11:15	Walk through
11:45	Lunch
12:45 p.m.	Individual meetings (flexible)
	Review opponent's video
1:30	Special teams meeting
2:00	Practice
4:15	Practice over
5:00	Coaches review practice video
	List openers
	Review script board and prepare cards for Friday practice
	Prepare scripts

FRIDAY

7:30 a.m.	Staff meeting
8:15	QB meeting
8:30	Special team meeting
9:00	Team meeting (5)
	Review practice video; OL separate
9:45	Offense reviews checks and alerts
10:00	Individual meetings
11:00	Practice
1:00 p.m.	Practice over
	Finalize offensive sideline sheet

SATURDAY

9:00 a.m.	Review practice video; O.L. separate
	Individual meetings
10:30	Practice
11:15	Practice over
6:00 -8:00 p.m.	Check into hotel
9:00 p.m.	Special teams meetings
9:30	Offensive/defensive meetings
	Use cut ups to support opening calls
	View game video to give players the flavor of the game plan and opponent's approach.
10:00	Team meeting
10:05	Snack

Practice Structure

The next step is to take a look at what we can realistically expect to practice in each situation and how best to proportion the time alloted to each section. To do this, we must first understand that very specific limits exist regarding the number of plays you can expect to efficiently practice in a given week. The best way to examine this issue is to evaluate several key factors:

- The length of your practice
- How are your practices divided between periods (individual, group, skeleton, and team)?
- What aspect of the offense is practiced in each period?

You would expect that the overall practice time would be divided up proportionately by the amount of offense used per situation. In reality, this proportion may not reflect the exact relationship to game calls, because certain situations are emphasized in a game more than others (i.e., Red Zone and third downs vs. base open-field offense).

If you do not identify each group/team period as a specific situation, I strongly suggest you do so. This step will help you to isolate exactly how much time you are spending in each area, and help your coaches and players focus on what is being called by situation. Whatever your particular practice structure consists of, it should be easy for you to look at that structure and determine how much time is being spent in group or team situations and how it should be broken down.

As has been pointed out several times already, I am not advocating that only one way exists to set up a practice structure or that such a structure should be based on a specific ratio. As a coach, It is your job as a coach to determine what best suits your needs and how much attention any offensive situational segment should receive. What I am advocating is that you should give substantial thought to what your particular offensive needs are and how you are you going to utilize each minute of your practice to meet those needs. When I was on Minnesota's staff, the Vikings' practice week broke down by situations as follows:

PRACTICE RATIO

DAY	PERIOD	BASE	3RD LONG	3RD MED	SY	BU	RED ZONE	GL	2PT	TOTAL	
WEDNESDAY	W.T.	10	3	3						16	
	INSIDE	6								6	
	TEAM	8								8	
	SKEL	6		4						10	
	TEAM	6	4							10	50
THURSDAY	W.T.	4			2	3	5	4	2	20	
	TEAM				2		5	4	2	13	
	SKELL	6	4				4			14	
	TEAM	7		4						11	58
FRIDAY	TEAM				2		5	3	2	12	
	SKELL		4				6			10	22
TOTALS		53	15	11	6	3	25	11	6	130	
		41%	12%	8%	5%	2%	19%	8%	5%		

Table 7-2. A breakdown of the Vikings' practice situations in 1995.

The numbers in Table 7-2 represent any scripted period against a live defense. What is not shown in this table are individual and group periods where we serviced ourselves. "W.T." is a walk through period we performed in shorts. The small number of snaps on Friday were due to the fact that during this practice, we used a team period to run a live two-minute drill and a separate team period to run a semi-live, "move-the-ball" drill where the head coach started us on the 30-yard line and gave us 8-10 situations to which we had to react.

I want to emphasize again that these ratios and formats are examples of the way we laid out our work week. Your priorities, time lines, and points of emphasis may be entirely different. The important point that needs to be made is the interactive way the total offensive package evolves directly in a proportional manner from game plan to practice structure to actual game calls.

Initially, the Vikings' offense practice numbers may seem substantially low to you. Keep in mind that we had only 53 players with which to work each week. As a result, we did not have the numbers that some college and high schools programs may have to provide entire scout teams to be sent off with their respective counterparts to practice for two full hours.

When I was growing up, the mentality and numbers involved with teams enabled football coaches to take large blocks of time and divide their team into separate offensive and defensive practices, each of which utilized the services of a complete scout team. With the reduction in the number of scholarships and the time limitations imposed on many collegiate programs today, the numbers available to college coaches have considerably diminished. As a result, more and more college teams are adapting their practice formats to those used in the NFL.

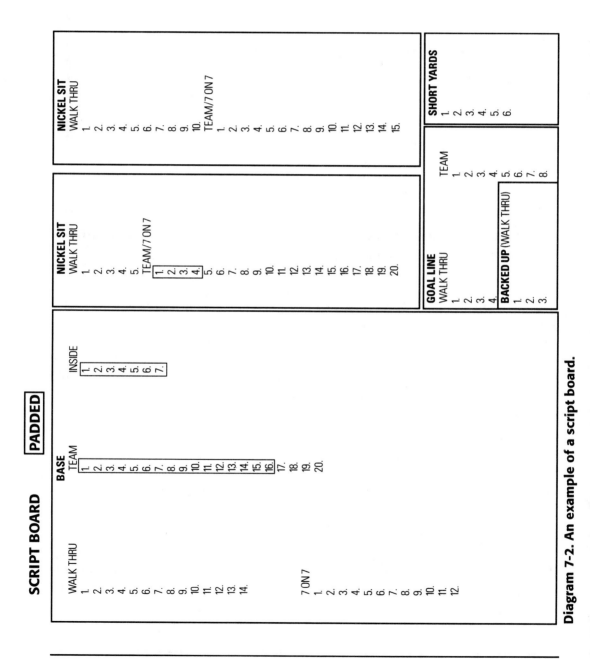

Diagram 7-2. An example of a script board.

Scripting

As was pointed out previously in the text, whatever the parameters you set for practiving, it is important to recognize that there is a finite limit to the amount of time you can effectively practice. Diagram 7-2 illustrates an example of the script board that sat next to the game plan board in the Vikings' offensive meeting room. It shows the total scripted snaps by each situation. By laying out the scripts on this board, you can, at a glance, check the total number of times you are running a given play, from what formations and against what defenses. The script board, like the game-plan board, gives each coach a reference point during the week as to what is being scripted, and when. This tool enables coaches to look at the entire week in one glance and use it for drawing their cards, or for preparing their meetings based on what and where the different parts of the offense are being installed.

Because of the limitations of the number of live snaps that can actually get done during the course of a week, we often prioritize what we think needs to be done vs a live defense and what can be run in a group or individual period. For example, if there is a route progression that we have run a great deal and the players are fairly proficient at, I may not script that route in one of our live periods. In this particular instance, I have decided that we are familiar enough with the route progression that I can brush it up in an individual or group period and save the live snaps for something new or something on which we may need extra work.

Training Camp Preparation

We use the same method of practice ratios in our training-camp preparation as we do during the season. Our training camp basically involves an initial week of preparation that culminates in a scrimmage and mock game. The next week then usually involves a scrimmage with another team, with the week ending with our first preseason game.

Diagram 7-3 illustrates how Minnesota alloted practice time to offensive situations during the Vikings' training camp in 1995. Because most college and high school teams have a similar two-week training camp period, the Vikings' numbers could easily be adjusted to reflect the totals you want to accomplish.

Coaching Assignments

How you utilize your staff when preparing and installing your game plan can be a major asset. It has been well documented that small interactive groups are a much better way to communicate and teach. Furthermore, the time and scope involved with establishing and implementing a game plan makes it very difficult for one individual to effectively do everything. I recognize that you probably don't have as many coaches to work with as we have in the NFL, but delegating responsibilities can be a very effective way of analyzing and formulating the best possible game plan. An example of the way we divided up our responsibilities when I was with the Vikings is illustrated in Diagram 7-4. As you can see, many tasks are divided between two people. Accordingly, if your numbers dictate, you could consolidate several of these functions.

VIKINGS' TRAINING CAMP PRACTICE ALLOTMENT — 1995

DAY	PRAC	TYPE	BASE TEAM	BASE SKEL	2ND LONG TEAM	2ND LONG SKEL	3RD LONG TEAM	3RD LONG SKEL	3RD MED TEAM	3RD MED SKEL	SHORT YARDAGE TEAM	SHORT YARDAGE SKEL	GOAL LINE TEAM	GOAL LINE SKEL	RED ZONE TEAM	RED ZONE SKEL	2 PT	BU
MON	1	SHELL	15	14	11	6	10	5	5	4								
MON	2	SHELL		6	5		5		4	6								
TUES	3	PADS	9	10	5	4												
TUES	4	SHORTS: SPECIAL TEAMS PRACTICE																
WED	5	PADS		10						2					10	8		
WED	6	SHORTS	4	4		4		4	6	4	4				8	12	2	5
THUR	7	PADS		4									5					
THUR	8	SHORTS: SPECIAL TEAMS PRACTICE																
FRI	9	SHORTS		10		4		4	4	2	4		6		4		2	5
FRI	10	PADS: SCRIMMAGE																
SAT	11	SHORTS: MOCK GAME																
MON	12	SHORTS	4	10	4		4		4	5					10	10	4	
MON	13	PADS	9	8	5				5	8					15	15		
TUES	14	SHELL		6		4				5								
TUES	15	PADS	6	10														
TOTALS			**47 / 139**	**92**	**30 / 52**	**22**	**19 / 32**	**13**	**28 / 64**	**36**	**8 / 8**	**0**	**11 / 11**	**0**	**47 / 92**	**45**		
WED	16	PADS	6	8			4	4	4									
WED	17	SHELLS: SPECIAL TEAMS PRACTICE																
THUR	18	PADS		5	4				4	5			5					
THUR	19	SHORTS	15	6					4		3							
FRI	20	PADS	6	5		4			4				4		4	3	2	
FRI	21	SHORTS: SPECIAL TEAMS PRACTICE																
SAT	22	SHELL	4						2	3	3		4		4		2	
SAT	23	SHORTS	4	5						4							4	0
TOTALS			**31 / 64**	**33**	**4 / 8**		**4 / 8**		**18 / 34**	**16**	**10 / 10**		**13 / 13**		**14 / 17**	**3**		

Diagram 7-3. A chart showing how the Vikings allotted practice time in training camp in 1995.

OFFENSIVE COACHES ASSIGNMENT CHART (1996)

Situations	Brian	Ray	Chip	Carl	Mike	Keith
Positions	Off-Coordinator	Quarterbacks	Wide Receivers	Running Backs	TE/OL	OL
Game Analysis	All situations	Nickel Pass Red Zone Pass Blitz	Nickel Pass Red Zone Pass Nickel catalog	Gen. Run Sy-GI Red Zone Run 4 minute Run	Computer Reports: Self Scout Opponent Analysis	Gen. Run Sy-GI Red Zone Run 4 minute Run
Scout Report	Game Plan Outline Route Sheets		Personnel Cover sheet	Fronts Run sheets Pro. sheets	Tendencies	Stunts Blitz [Front/Sy/GI(Tape)]
Week	Scripts	Pass Play Coverages Team Cards Blitz Period [Blitz Tape]	Pass Play Coverages Scout Teams Cov.	Compile Cards Group Run Cards	Walk Thru Cards Spec. Cat Cards Scouts Fronts	Team Cards 9-7 Cards Blitz Cards [Sy-GI-2 Pt Tape]
Game	Play calling	Secondary	Substition	Call Chart	Front	P.O.A
Half-Time	Coordinate 2nd Half focus and calls Address Off.	Compile Pass Recom. Meet with QB	Meet with WR	Meet with RB	Situation Chart- Compile Run Recom. Meet with TE	Meet with OL

Diagram 7-4. An example of an offensive coaches assignment chart.

Summary Points

The key elements in establishing your plan for installing your offense are:

- Consolidate each situation and determine the size of each package.

- Be very aware of how much overage you have in each area. The ratio of what you need vs. what can be practiced is vital.

- Structure your game plan discussions and layout so that everyone is on the same page as to what is being done.

- Don't be afraid to delegate responsibilities for different aspects of the game plan.

- Make sure at week's end you have practiced what you had intended to practice and have covered all that you have needed to cover.

- Make sure each coach knows what he is responsible for during the game.

CHAPTER 8

Game Day

Two of the most important aspects of finishing a game plan are how it is laid out for game day calls and how members of the coaching staff approach their assignments on game day. How a coach lays out his game plan for game day calls is a very subjective matter. It is usually developed after years of trial and error and having laid things out in just a certain way to meet a particular objective. Often the layout is less a function of organization than it is personal preference.

Keep in mind that the game-day layout of the offense has to function for the rest of the coaching staff as well. So far, several points have been made in this book about the best game plans being ones that are interactive with both coaches and players. As a result, it follows that the actual layout of a game plan should also serve the purposes of all those involved.

The point has also been made that even though a coach may work very hard to organize the game to flow in a certain manner, things sometimes go awry. Accordingly, the game plan must be laid out so that you can access the plan that was practiced during the week and utilize the plays and formations you prepared, even if it is not quite in the sequence or ratio you had hoped. For this reason, our game plans are laid out in three sections:

- Sequenced and situation calls

- Play or special situation

- Formation and personnel

Even if the game goes according to plan, you may need to make occasional sequential adjustments within the game plan to take advantage of certain plays that seem to be working well or formations and personnel groups that seem to give the defense problems. If the game is not going along in the sequence you had hoped for, you must be able to access what you have practiced during the week. This situation is an instance where your manner of laying out the game plan is vitally important. If you do not have it laid out in an organized and efficient way, you may end up discarding your plan (and all the work you put into it during the week) and having to simply wing it.

An example of a type of game-day sheet that the Vikings used when I was on Minnesota's staff is illustrated in Diagram 8-1. On the far left of this sheet are the situational calls that have been scripted during the week. These are listed in the order I want to call them and are presented to the team in the two meetings on the day before the game.

The center section of the game-day sheet is little more than a listing of plays by type: run, pass, play action, screens, etc. It also lists the plays in special categories that are not a part of your normal play-calling sequence on the left.

On the right side of the game-plan sheet are the same plays listed by personnel and formations. This sheet is given to the players earlier in the week. This step allows them to prepare with a little more focus on what plays are going to be run by which personnel, so that those players who may make their major contribution to the game through special plays or formations can focus on those particular plays in those specific groupings.

Coaching Assignments

This aspect can be one of the more difficult parts of implementing a game plan. In reality, it can be hard for some coaches to avoid getting caught up in the action and become spectators who watch the game. As such, it is important that each coach be given a specific assignment and that he maintain his focus on his particular job. We have all been in situations where a player thinks something happened a certain way, when in fact it did not. If you chastise a player for being wrong because you thought you saw it differently, when in fact it was the way the player saw it, not only have you not helped him adjust during the game, but that player may lose a little confidence in your abilities. For this reason, we give each coach a specific part of the play to watch and be accountable for. On the Vikings staff, we assigned observation responsibilities as follows:

- *Receivers coach:*
  Watches secondary for coverages, rotations, and match ups.

- *Running backs coach:*
  Watches backfield action for the ball exchange and the drop of quarterback.

- *Tight ends coach:*
  Watches and charts the total front.

- *Offensive line coach:*
  Watches the point of attack.

DATE	OPPONENT				Per/Formation
Openers	1st/2nd Down	Base Runs	Base Pass	Cov 2	(R) Far/Dot
	3rd Med	Draws	Quicks		(T) Sprd/Slot
	3rd and Long	Nickel Run	Play Action	Blitz	(T) Twins
Short Yardage	End Zone	Screen	Action Pass		(3) Dbl
Red Zone (+20)	3rd Down	Specials		Best Player	(3) Train
(+15)	Goal Line	2 Minute	Backed Up		(3) Bunch/Vice
	Pressure	4 Minute			
	2 Pts	Last 3 Plays	2 Point Chart		
	+10				

Diagram 8-1. Sample game-day sheet.

In this way, our offensive staff can cover a play from all angles. As a result, if a player is confused or makes a mistake, we can have a legitimate answer for him as to what actually happened and what should have happened.

CHAPTER 9

The Soap Box

This chapter is named, "The Soap Box," because it involves some personal perspectives on the direction that our profession is going and some coaching aids available to you that I steadfastly advocate. One of the points that I feel very strongly about is that we have reached the threshold of a veritable explosion of computer technologies that are available, affordable and functional. No one can reasonably deny that every aspect of our lives is being affected by computers. Equally undeniable is the fact that there is no aspect of professional interaction that can be done more quickly, more efficiently, with more organization and more professionally, than with the use of the computer.

Too often people have resisted the technological wave of advancement, thinking that a computer is nothing more than a number-crunching, dehumanizing, complicated mechanism—a device intended for either only the most sophisticated "hackers" or for the games of children. Nothing could be further from the truth.

The very term "computer" is a misnomer. "Communicator" would be a more applicable name to describe what the computer can potentially do for you in our profession. Generally speaking, three areas exist where a coach can genuinely affect the performance of his players and where most advancements in philosophies and principles have occured:

- Physical training methods
- Fundamental knowledge (techniques and strategies)
- Teaching methods

In the area of physical training, the body of knowledge has consistently grown over the years with regard to how diet and exercise can enhance a player's on-the-field performance. Fortunately, much of this information can easily be passed on to your athletes as it becomes available.

Furthermore, the body of fundamental knowledge concerning the game has also over the years gone through regular transformations with regard to what are the best techniques and strategies available. In fact, the game has not changed in this regard for quite some time. What changes actually take place tend to not be innovative so much as they are cyclical. By this, I mean that styles and tactics go in and out of vogue based on who has won the last Super Bowl. An example of what I am referring to is the famous counter trey play utilized by Joe Gibbs in the Super Bowl days of the Washington Redskins.

The counter trey is a fundamentally sound play that almost all teams have used in one form or another since the mid-80s. As is usually the case, defenses have seen it enough now that they can play the counter very effectively. As a result, the success of this series has diminished somewhat. As the play begins to fade from playbooks to the point that no one really runs it, defenses will next move on to addressing whatever offensive series has taken its place. What the time frame is I can not say for certain, but eventually someone will "re-invent" the counter trey, and because teams have not seen it for awhile, it will again be very successful. Most fundamentals and strategies follow this type of cycle.

That leaves us with the actual teaching methods that we employ as being the one true area where the most innovations are taking place. It is my opinion that it is this area where you can best gain the "edge" that all coaches are constantly looking for to enhance their chances of winning.

I mentioned earlier that I thought one of the keys to Bill Walsh's "West Coast Offense" was less in the actual X's and O's than it was in the innovative approaches he took in installing and implementing those fundamentals. Coach Walsh's offense is a beautifully conceived structure that has had unparalleled success. But those who simply copy the plays used in the system are not able to duplicate its success if they do not take into account the teaching progression that accompanies it.

This point brings me back to my original "soap box". Computers/communicators provide us with an exciting new means with which to coach/teach our players. When I joined the Vikings' staff in 1992, there was not a single PC used by any member of the coaching staff. Today virtually every coach in the NFL has one. Even an old-style diehard coach like Bill Parcells in his book, *Finding a Way to Win*, says, "If the competition has laptop computers and you're still using yellow legal pads, it won't matter how long and hard you work, they're going to pass you by."

At this point, I'd like to present a couple of ways we use the PC in our game-plan preparation that may prompt some workable ideas for you and your program. First, most coaches have some form of a game-analysis program that they use to collate and summarize their opponents' tendencies. In some cases, this program is interfaced with video that is set up to generate forms of cut-up tapes either for analysis or for teaching purposes.

Short of this you can utilize just a regular spreadsheet from any basic program such as Lotus or Excel. By keeping your game analysis or self-scout material in this manner, you can very easily and quickly look at any specific aspect of your opponent's defense or your own offense to help you make a play-calling decision during the course of your preparation.

For example, if you are interested in running a certain route in 3rd-and-4-6 and you wanted to check when the last time you ran that progression or how this week's opponent defended this formation in this situation, you could easily find that specific information by sorting the proper categories on your spreadsheet (Figure 9-1). Often, there are specific questions you may have that a larger, more encompassing game-analysis report may not sufficiently cover. The time and effort to go back and look at all the film for that specific example may discourage you from finding out the information you need. A spreadsheet can make that process much quicker and more efficient.

GM	#	DN	DIST	POS.	PER	SHFT	FORMATION	VAR	MOT	PLAY	DISCRIPTION	C/I	#	GAIN	DP	DEF	COV	SNT	BLZ
PIT	1	1	10	-24	R		DOT		HUMP	LIZ	DALLAS	C	87	4	R	UN	1		
PIT	2	1	5	-29	T	SHAFT	TRIPS		ZAP	70	WAGGLE	C	80	8	R	UN	3S		
PIT	3	1	10	-37	R		DOT		HUMP	50	ISO		26	3	R	UN	1		
PIT	4	2	7	-40	T		TRIPS		ZM	BLUE	ORLANDO	I	86	0			1D		D
PIT	5	3	7	-40	3		DBL			LO	479 R FLAT	I	82	0	D	OV	5H		
PIT	6	1	10	-6	T		SPRD	SLOT		50	GUT		26	7	R	UN	3		
PIT	7	2	3	-13	T		TRIPS		WIZ	RIP	DETROIT	C	80	10	R	UN	1		
PIT	8	1	10	-23	T		SPRD		ZM	50	GUT		26	10	R	UN	1		
PIT	9	1	10	-35	H		SQZ			70	CHIP		26	2	R	OV	88		
PIT	10	2	8	-37	3		DBL			RIP	DODGE DBL	C	80	9	R	34	2	X	ZD
PIT	11	1	10	-46	H		SQZ			RED	DETROIT	C	86	12	R	34	4S		
PIT	12	1	10	42	T		TWIN			70	CHIP		26	1	R	34	1		
PIT	13	2	9	41	T		TWIN			FL	099	I	86	0	R	UN	88		

Figure 9-1. Sample spreadsheet for sorting and presenting detailed play-call data.

Another way the PC can be used is to draw all of your plays (runs, passes, protections, defenses) and organize catalogues with these schematics for future use. For years, coaches have spent countless hours diagramming plays and formations. In many cases, these plays are the same ones drawn up over and over in the same way. By cataloging our schematics, you can make whatever subtle changes you may need a particular opponent and lay it out for the players to have quickly and with a great deal more detail.

For example, the schematics shown in Figure 9-2 were done with basic draw programs like Super Paint, Intellidraw, or Visio. Most word processing programs, like PageMaker, Word Perfect, and Microsoft Word, have this type of basic drawing capability.

All of our scripting is done on a spreadsheet that allows us to sort by play and by defense to check our teaching progression and make sure we have covered each play against the proper defensive looks. The spreadsheets in Figure 9-3 illustrate the comprehensive data that can be provided to coaches.

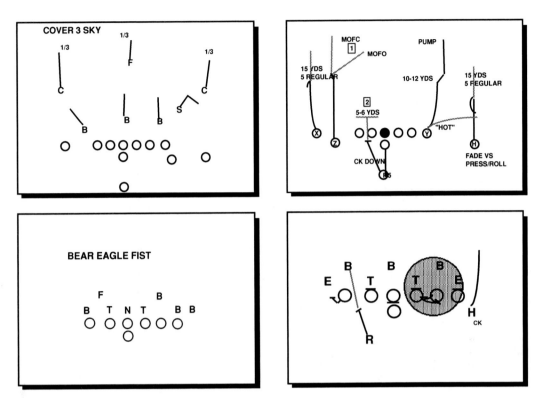

Figure 9-2. Sample schematics drawn with a computer.

Furthermore, by sorting all of your plays by type, formation, and personnel on these spreadshets, you can provide your players with an excellent resource to establish the game plan by whichever way they prefer to learn it. Some players feel that the personnel-and-formation breakdown is the best way to learn, while others (like the quarterbacks) prefer to internalize the plays when they are grouped by type. Figure 9-4 illustrates the two primary methods of sorting plays.

Two other technological advances that are currently available that have the potential to be very useful tools for coaches are CD-ROM technology and DVD technology. Both types of technology allow you to take the concept of sorting your plays or your game analysis on a spreadsheet and enhance that capability by being able to sort and view the actual video of those plays in the same manner and with the same speed. Right now, the only limitation to either CD-ROM or DVD technology is to make it cost effective enough to make it affordable on the mass market.

In the future, I strongly believe that books of this nature will be accompanied by either a CD-ROM or a DVD disk that will allow you to access further information on any particular topic in this medium, or to call up video examples of what is being discussed.

OPPONENT: CINCINNATI   DATE:

NO.	SIT.	HS	P	FORMATION	PLAY	DISCRIPT	DEF
16	3RD 4	M	4	ROCKET RT	20	BRUSH 'A'	41 - 88
8	GROUP RUN		R	FAR LT SP	70	CHIP	43W
7	GROUP RUN		R	FAR LT SP	70	CHIP	EV
4	BASE		R	FAR LT SP	70	CHIP	EVEN - 2
6	GROUP RUN		R	FAR LT SPEAR	70	CHIP	UNDER - 3 SKY
5	RZ +15	L	H	FAR LT WG	70	CHIP	OV 88
4	RZ +20	R	H	FAR RT WG	60	CHIP	56 WIDE 3
5	GROUP RUN		R	NEAR RT ZEKE	60	CHIP	43 - 2
9	GROUP RUN		R	NR RT	60	CHIP	EV
4	BASE		R	NR RT ZEKE	60	CHIP	UNDER - 2
1	3RD 1	M	J	DOT LT	70	CHIP SOLID	43 SMACK 3
1	3RD 1	M	J	DOT LT	70	CHIP SOLID	56 WIDE 3
5	3RD 1	M	J	DOT LT	70	CHIP SOLID	EAGLE 2
13	GL	M	J	DOT LT F. ZM	70	CHIP SOLID	62 -0
10	GL	M	J	DOT LT F. ZM	70	CHIP SOLID	62 -0
8	GL	M	J	DOT RT F. ZM	60	CHIP SOLID	62 -0
4	BASE		R	FAR LT	30	CUTBACK	UNDER - 3 SKY
8	RZ +20	R	H	FAR RT WG	20	CUTBACK	56 WIDE 3
6	RZ +10	R	H	FAR RTWG	20	CUTBACK	EAGLE 2
2	BASE		R	NR RT WIZ	20	CUTBACK	EVEN - 4 SKY
4	GROUP RUN		R	FAR RT	40	GUT	56
20	BK UP		R	FAR RT	40	GUT	EVEN - 4 SKY
4	BASE		R	NR LT WIZ	50	GUT	EVEN - 2
3	GROUP RUN		R	NR LT WIZ	50	GUT	UN
1	BASE		R	ZOOM FAR RT	40	GUT	43 WIDE-3SKY TO 2
2	BASE		ZE	ZM TRAIN RT	60	H BEHIND	42 - 2
1	BASE		R	NEAR RT	40	ISO	EVEN - 2
2	GROUP RUN		R	FAR LT SP			
5	BASE		R	FAR RT SP			
1	GROUP RUN		R	NR RT			
8	BASE		R	NEAR LT			
15	GL	M	J	DOT RT F. ZM			
11	GL	M	J	DOT RT F. ZM			
12	GL	M	J	DOT RT F. ZM			
10	GL	M	J	FOT RT F. ZM			
8	GL	M	J	DOT RT F. ZM			
3	BASE		3	DBL LT FK SP			
11	GROUP RUN		3	DBL RT			
10	GROUP RUN		3	DBL RT			
11	GROUP RUN		3	DBL LT			

OPPONENT: CINCINNATI   DATE: WED NOV 8

WALK THRU

NO.	SIT.	HS	P	FORMATION	PLAY	DISCRIPT	DEF
1	BASE	R	R	FAR LT	SCAT LT	816 Y SEAM RM	43 UNDER - 2
2	BASE	L	R	NR RT WIZ	20	CB	EVEN - 4 SKY
3	BASE	L	R	FAR RT	RED	ORLANDO	43 OVER - 3
4	BASE	R	R	NR RT ZEKE	60	CHIP	UNDER - 2
5	BASE	L	R	FAR RT SP	40	ISO	UNDER - 2
6	BASE	R	E	TRN RT HIP	90	WAGGLE	UN NIC - 3S
7	BASE	R	ZE	DBL LT L. SP	RIP	DALLAS	42 NIC - 88
8	BASE	L	R		50	SLIDE 'A'	UNDER - 2
9	BASE	R	3	DBL LT	SCAT LT	H ANGLE DRAG	43 OV NIC - 2
10	BASE	L	3	DBL LT	70	TREY	42 - 88
11	3RD 4	L	3	DBL LT	HI	GIANT	ZN DOG OV NIC - 3
12	3RD 4	R	ZE	TRN LT F. WZ	SCAT LT	816 Y SEAM	UNDER NIC - 8
13	3RD 4	L	E	SPLIT RT	JET RT	DBL DODGE	42 NIC - 3
14	3RD 4	R	4	ROCKET RT F. LP	SPRT LT	JUKE	41 DIME - 8
15	3RD 4	M	4	ROCKET RT	60	VEER 'A'	41 - 88
16	3RD 4	M	4	ROCKET RT	20	BRUSH 'A'	41 - 88

GROUP RUN

NO.	SIT.	HS	P	FORMATION	PLAY	DISCRIPT	DEF
1	GROUP RUN		R	FAR RT	50	SLIDE	UN
2	GROUP RUN		R	FAR LT	40	SLIDE √ GA. GREEN	OV
3	GROUP RUN		R	NR LT WIZ	50	GUT	UN
4	GROUP RUN		R	FAR RT	40	GUT √ OPP.	56
5	GROUP RUN		R	FAR RT	60	OUT	43UN
6	GROUP RUN		R	NR LT WIZ	70	OUT √ OPP.	43 $ UP
7	GROUP RUN		R	FAR LT SP	70	CHIP √ SLIDE GRN.	EV
8	GROUP RUN		R	FAR LT SP	70	CHIP	43W
9	GROUP RUN		R	NR RT	60	CHIP / √ SLIDE YELLOW	EV
10	GROUP RUN		3	DBL RT	14	O'	56
11	GROUP RUN		3	DBL LT	15	O' √ PASS	43UN
12	GROUP RUN		3	DBL LT	20	TREY √ OMAHA YELLOW	43UN

SPECIAL CAT

NO.	SIT.	HS	P	FORMATION	PLAY	DISCRIPT	DEF
1	BASE	L	R	ZOOM FAR RT	40	GUT √	43 WIDE-3SKY TO 2
2	BASE	R	R	NEAR LT WIZ	40	SLIDE 'A'	43 UNDER - 2
3	BASE	L	ZE	BUNCH RT	90	WAGGLE	UNDER NIC - 2
4	BASE	R	R	FAR LT SP	70	CHIP	EVEN - 2
5	BASE	R	ZE	TRN LT	OPT	724	42 NIC - 1 LURK
6	BASE	R	3	DBL RT	30	TREY 'A'	UN NIC - 88
7	BASE	R	ZE	BUNCH RT	OPT RT	WACO	UNDER NIC - 3S
8	BASE	R	R	NEAR LT	50	ISO	UNDER - 2

Figure 9-3. Sample spreadsheets.

PLAYS BY TYPE

P	FORMATION	PLAY	DISCRIPT
4	ROCKET	20	BRUSH
R	FAR	20	CB
R	NEAR WIZ	20	CB
R	FAR SP	60	CHIP
H	WING FAR	60	CHIP
R	NEAR	60	CHIP
J	DOT -F. ZM	60	CHIP SOLID
H	WING FAR	20	CUTBACK
E	CHANGE	20	DRAW
R	FAR	40	GUT √
R	NEAR WIZ	40	GUT √
ZE	TRAIN ZM	60	H BEHIND
J	DOT F. ZM	20	LEAD
J	DOT F. ZM	40	LEAD O
3	DBL	14	O
R	FAR	60	OUTSIDE
R	NEAR WIZ	60	OUTSIDE
3	DBL	20	PAINT 'A'
3	TRAIN	20	PAINT 'A'
E	CHANGE	40	SLIDE 'A'
R	FAR	40	SLIDE 'A'
R	NEAR WIZ	40	SLIDE 'A'
H	WING JUG	40	SLIDE √
3	DBL	20	TREY 'A'
3	TRAIN	20	TREY 'A'
3	DBL	60	TREY 'A'
4	ROCKET	20	VEER
4	ROCKET	60	VEER
3	DBL EX	QB	WEDGE 'A'

P	FORMATION	PLAY	DISCRIPT
ZE	BUNCH L. WIZ	SPRINT	19
3	DBL	SPRINT	19
R	NEAR ZAP SHAFT	SPRINT	19
ZE	DBL L. SP	R/L	DALLAS
R	FAR SP	R/L	DALLAS
3	SPREAD SLOT SP	R/L	DALLAS
4	TRAIN	R/L	DALLAS
ZE	DBL SP	R/L	DENVER
4	ROCKET SP	R/L	DENVER
R	FAR SP	QK OPT	DETROIT
R	FAR (ZM)	R/B	ORLANDO
R	FAR SP	R/B	ORLANDO
H	WING	KICK	√
E	SPLIT	JET	DBL DODGE
4	ROCKET	SCAT	DBL DODGE
R	NEAR ZAP SHAFT	SCAT	FORD
3	DBL	H/L	GIANT
3	TRAIN	OPT	GIANT
3	DBL	SCRAM	44/55
3	DBL F. SP	SCAT	H ANGLE DRAG
R	FAR (ZM)	SCAT	H ANGLE DRAG
4	ROCKET	SCAT	H ANGLE DRAG
E	CHANGE	SCAT	R ANGLE
R	CHANGE	SCAT	R ANGLE
ZE	BUNCH L. WZ	F/L	DIG
4	TRAIN	SCAT	DIG Y SEAM X 8

P	FORMATION	PLAY	DISCRIPT
3	TRAIN	SPEED	JUKE
3	DBL	SPRINT	JUKE
4	ROCKET F. LP	SPRINT	JUKE
ZE	BUNCH	90	WAGGLE
ZE	TRAIN HIP	90	WAGGLE
E	SPLIT	90	WAGGLE SP
3	BUNCH	JET	SCREEN
E	SPLIT	JET	SCREEN
ZE	TRAIN F. WZ	SCRAM	7
ZE	TRAIN	OPT	495
ZE	TRAIN	OPT	599
ZE	TRAIN	OPT	724
3	TRAIN	OPT	748
ZE	TRIPS ZEKE	F/L	788
3	TRAIN	OPT	989
E	CHANGE	BASE	383 D. T.O
ZE	GANG SP	SCRAM	4 PIVOT M
3	DBL	H/L	585 D. CB
E	CHANGE	BASE	599 R FLAT
R	FAR SP	SCRAM	7M
4	ROCKET	SCAT	989 D. CROSS
ZE	DBL SP EX	QK SPRINT	DBL PIVOT
E	CHANGE	BASE	DIVIDE R FLAT
ZE	GANG SP	F/L	O88
ZE	DBL HIP	FK 80	SWEEP PASS
ZE	BUNCH WIZ	SCRAM	TD M

PLAYS BY PER/FORMATION

P	FORMATION	PLAY	DISCRIPT
3	BUNCH	JET	SCREEN
3	DBL	14	O
3	DBL	20	PAINT 'A'
3	DBL	20	TREY 'A'
3	DBL	60	TREY 'A'
3	DBL	SPRINT	19
3	DBL	H/L	GIANT
3	DBL	SCRAM	44/55
3	DBL	SPRINT	JUKE
3	DBL	H/L	585 D. CB
3	DBL EX	QB	WEDGE 'A'
3	DBL F. SP	SCAT	H ANGLE DRAG
3	SPREAD SLOT SP	R/L	DALLAS
3	TRAIN	20	PAINT 'A'
3	TRAIN	20	TREY 'A'
3	TRAIN	OPT	GIANT
3	TRAIN	SPEED	JUKE
3	TRAIN	OPT	748
3	TRAIN	OPT	989

P	FORMATION	PLAY	DISCRIPT
4	ROCKET	20	BRUSH
4	ROCKET	20	VEER
4	ROCKET	60	VEER
4	ROCKET	SCAT	DBL DODGE
4	ROCKET	SCAT	H ANGLE DRAG
4	ROCKET	SCAT	989 D. CROSS
4	ROCKET F. LP	SPRINT	JUKE
4	ROCKET SP	R/L	DENVER
4	TRAIN	R/L	DALLAS
4	TRAIN	SCAT	DIG Y SEAM X 8

P	FORMATION	PLAY	DISCRIPT
ZE	BUNCH	90	WAGGLE
ZE	BUNCH L. WIZ	SPRINT	19
ZE	BUNCH L. WZ	F/L	DIG
ZE	BUNCH OV	OPT	WACO
ZE	BUNCH WIZ	SCRAM	TD M
ZE	DBL HIP	FK 80	SWEEP PASS
ZE	DBL L. SP	R/L	DALLAS
ZE	DBL SP	R/L	DENVER
ZE	DBL SP EX	QK SPRT	DBL PIVOT
ZE	GANG	H/L	ZIPPER
ZE	GANG SP	SCRAM	4 PIVOT M
ZE	GANG SP	F/L	O88
ZE	TRAIN	OPT	495
ZE	TRAIN	OPT	599
ZE	TRAIN	OPT	724
ZE	TRAIN F. WIZ	SCAT	816 Y SEAM
ZE	TRAIN F. WZ	SCRAM	7
ZE	TRAIN HIP	90	WAGGLE
ZE	TRAIN ZM	60	H BEHIND
ZE	TRIPS ZEKE	F/L	788

P	FORMATION	PLAY	DISCRIPT
R	CHANGE	SCAT	R ANGLE
R	FAR	20	CB
R	FAR	40	GUT √
R	FAR	60	OUTSIDE
R	FAR	40	SLIDE 'A'
R	FAR (RM)	SCAT	816 Y SEAM
R	FAR (ZM)	R/B	ORLANDO
R	FAR (ZM)	SCAT	H ANGLE DAG
R	FAR SP	60	CHIP
R	FAR SP	R/L	DALLAS
R	FAR SP	QK OPT	DETROIT
R	FAR SP	R/B	ORLANDO
R	FAR SP	SCRAM	7M
R	NEAR	60	CHIP
R	NEAR WIZ	20	CB
R	NEAR WIZ	40	GUT √
R	NEAR WIZ	60	OUTSIDE
R	NEAR WIZ	40	SLIDE 'A'
R	NEAR ZAP SHFT	SPRINT	19
R	NEAR ZAP SHFT	SCAT	FORD

P	FORMATION	PLAY	DISCRIPT
E	CHANGE	20	DRAW
E	CHANGE	40	SLIDE 'A'
E	CHANGE	SCAT	R ANGLE
E	CHANGE	BASE	599 R FLAT
E	CHANGE	BASE	DIVIDE R FLAT
E	CHANGE (SWAP)	SCAT	816 Y SEAM
E	SPLIT	JET	D. DODGE
E	SPLIT	90	WAGGLE SP
E	SPLIT	JET	SCREEN
3	CHANGE	BASE	383 D. T.O

P	FORMATION	PLAY	DISCRIPT
H	WING FAR	60	CHIP
H	WING FAR	20	CUTBACK
H	WING JUG	40	SLIDE √
H	WING	KICK	√

P	FORMATION	PLAY	DISCRIPT
J	DOT -F. ZM	60	CHIP SLD
J	DOT F. ZM	20	LEAD
J	DOT F. ZM	40	LEAD O
J	DOT F. ZM	PP 60	Z FLAT

Figure 9-4. Examples of two basic methods for sorting plays.

With the NCAA-mandated limitations regarding how much time college athletes can spend with the coaching staff in the off-season, you can easily see the potential teaching benefits of a player being able to come by the football office to pick up a disk that he can take home and view on his own. Such a disk may contain a certain series of plays that you want to cover with the athlete, accompanied by printed material, video support, and even videotape of you explaining the series.

If any of this seems far fetched, simply take a stroll over to the computer lab that virtually every school in the nation has on its campus and look at the way these very teaching tools are already being used. If you were ever looking for that little "edge" that might give you the extra dimension you need to make your team just that much better, believe me this is it.

CHAPTER 10

Closing Points

Hopefully, this book has provided you with some insight into a meaningful and efficient way that you can systematically structure and develop your offensive game plans.

The following 10 key points summarize what I have attempted to share with you in this book:

1) You must clearly identify what your responsibilities are as the offensive coordinator (play caller) of your team.

2) You must constantly analyze the methods you are using to implement your game plan and determine the capabilities of the group of players you are dealing with each year.

3) Determining the size and scope of the offense you wish to run in any given year or game is the single most important aspect of developing your game plan.

4) In creating your game plan, you should keep the four key measures of turnovers, explosive plays, 1st down efficiency ,and Red Zone efficiency in mind.

5) You should establish an opening sequence that can be identified, practiced, and implemented by the entire coaching staff and offensive team.

6) You should identify the parameters of every situational offensive segment and identify the measurable success of each segment and how you are going to achieve those levels of success.

7) You should have a plan for every conceivable contingency your team will face, no matter how unusual the circumstances may seem.

8) You should be as detailed and specific as your time and materials allow.

9) You should make sure you are using all the tools available to you.

10) You should recognize that the most important factor in your game plan is the human element, and that the way you interact with your coaches and players affects any and all preparations you make.

The main points covered in each chapter were as follows:

Introduction

The key elements in developing your offensive package are:

- Define your job as "offensive coordinator" and the approach you will take.

- Recognize that above all else you are a teacher and determine the capabilities of your students/players and the best methods of teaching/coaching them.

- Keep in mind that preparing any game plan involves four main elements:

    ✓ Determining size and scope of the offense
    ✓ Outline situational offensive needs
    ✓ Implementation of game plan
    ✓ Game-day needs

- Remember that the number one element in approaching each of the aforementioned four areas is to be as detailed and specific as your time and materials allow.

- Keep the four "key" measurable categories in mind when formulating your game-plan:

    ✓ Turnovers
    ✓ Explosive plays
    ✓ First-down efficiency
    ✓ Red Zone efficiency

How Much Offense?

The key elements in determining how much offense you should carry are:

- Think on three levels when determining how much offense you can run: yearly, weekly, and on game day.

- Take the time to determine exactly the size and scope of each critical situation you will face.

- Work hard to keep your overage of plays to 25-30%.

- Take the time to review each week the amount and nature of offense you ran and see if your planning stayed within the expected norms you set for yourself.

Base Offense

The key elements in establishing your base offense are:

- Determine size and scope of the package you need.

- Determine if a recognizable difference exists between first down and 2nd-and-long.

- Establish an opening sequence and be specific with regard to what you want to run and then stick by it.

- Keep your opening sequences interactive with regard to personnel and formations.

- Keep your opening priorities in mind:

    ✓ Get a first down
    ✓ Keep yourself in a convertible third-down distance
    ✓ Create an "explosive"

Third Down

The key elements in establishing your third-down package are:

- Determine the size and scope of your package.

- Recognize the success ratio you can expect in each phase:

    ✓ 3rd-and-long   (20-25%)
    ✓ 3rd-and-medium   (45-50%)
    ✓ 3rd-and-short   (75-85%)

- Leave your options open for your quarterback and be certain he understands what those options are.

- Have a plan to handle the blitz.

- Match your plays by personnel and formation.

- Determine your plan for 3rd-and-short during the week and stay with your plan.

Pre-Red Zone and Red Zone

The key elements in establishing your Red Zone package are:

- Determine the size and scope of your package.

- Determine the abilities of your kicking game, and once inside field-goal range, never put yourself in position to be taken out of that range.

- Remember that this is an area where you must have the most detailed part of your game plan and should eliminate as many "surprises" as you can.

- Coordinate your +10, goal line, and two-point plan to be interactive, be prepared to carry one aspect of the plan into the other.

Special Category

The key elements in establishing your special category package are:

- Determine the size and scope of each package, even if it is unlikely it will come up.

- Coach your players to understand the unique properties of each of these situations.

- Stress the importance of each situation and reinforce the fact that it may come down to one of these situations to win a game.

- Make sure that the players know your intentions in each of these situations and that they do not misinterpret your actions in these situations as a sign of panic.

Installation and Game Plan

The key elements in establishing your installation are:

- Consolidate each situation and determine the size of each package.

- Be very aware of how much overage you have in each area. The ratio of what you need vs. what can be practiced is vital.

- Structure your game-plan discussions and layout so that everyone is on the same page as to what is being done.

- Don't be afraid to delegate responsibilities for different aspects of the game plan.

- Make sure at week's end you have practiced what you had intended to practice and have covered all that you have needed to cover.

- Make sure each coach knows what he is responsible for during the game.

A Commitment to Winning

The very fact that you are reading this book indicates that you are one of those types of individuals who is constantly looking to improve your craft and be the best coach and teacher that you can be. I commend you for your efforts and hope that this material might be of some small help in your endeavor to prepare a winning football team.

Brian Billick is the former head coach of the Baltimore Ravens, a position he held for nine seasons (1999-2007). In 2001, he led Baltimore to the penultimate victory, capturing Super Bowl XXXV, 34-7, over the New York Giants. One of the most knowledgeable and articulate coaches in the game, Billick has been an NFL game analyst on FOX since 2008.

Before accepting the reins of the Ravens' program, Billick served as the offensive coordinator for the Minnesota Vikings from 1994-'98. Highly successful, he was the architect of a Vikings' attack that set a variety of NFL and team records in a 15-1 1998 campaign. Over his five full seasons, Billick guided the Vikings into the top five in the NFL in yards per game, passing yards per game, completions and third-down conversions. Under Billick's guidance, the Vikings recorded their top three offensive seasons (1998, 1995 and 1994), and five of the top 10 offensive seasons in team history. Most importantly, the Vikings advanced to the playoffs all but one season (1995) during Billick's tenure. Minnesota played postseason games in 1993-'94 and 1996-'98.

Before his appointment with the Vikings, Brian was a Stanford assistant from 1989-'91 under Coach Dennis Green. He helped in the development of wide receivers Ed McCaffrey and Chris Walsh and tight ends Ryan Wetnight and Jim Price. All four went on to NFL careers. Prior to Stanford, Billick spent three seasons as offensive coordinator at Utah State (1986-'88). Brian helped develop quarterback Brent Snyder, who set school passing marks with 2,887 yards in 1987 and 3,218 yards in 1988. When he arrived at Utah State, the team was ranked 107th out of 108 NCAA Division 1-A teams offensively. In his final two seasons as Utah State's offensive coordinator, the Aggies ranked in the top 10 in total offense.

Brian began his coaching career as an assistant at the University of the Redlands in 1977, while helping coach a local high school team at the same time. He spent the following year (1978) as a graduate assistant at Brigham Young University. At BYU, he worked with tight ends and the offensive line. Following that season, Brian was assistant director of public relations for the San Francisco 49ers in 1979-'80. Two years earlier (1977), Billick had been drafted by the 49ers in the 11th round, was released; and had a brief stint with the Dallas Cowboys. Brian earned All-Western Athletic Conference honors and honorable mention All-America in 1976 as a tight end at Brigham Young University. In 1976, he caught 20 passes for 338 yards and a touchdown. Brian played linebacker at Air Force as a freshman before transferring to BYU.

Born in Fairborne, Ohio, Billick earned three letters in football and basketball, and was a Helms Scholar-Athlete as a senior at Redlands (CA) High School. Brian and his wife, Kim, have two daughters, Aubree and Keegan.